Forever Changed

Forever Changed

A Story of God's Transforming Power

Teresa Kemp

BROWN
CHRISTIAN PRESS
A DIVISION OF
BROWN BOOKS PUBLISHING

All Scripture quotations, unless otherwise noted, are taken from the *Amplified Bible* ©1987 by the Zondervan Corporation.

Forever Changed
A Story of God's Transforming Power

Brown Christian Press
16250 Knoll Trail Drive, Suite 205
Dallas, Texas 75248
www.BrownChristianPress.com
(972) 381-0009

A New Era in Publishing™

ISBN 978-1-61254-185-3
LCCN 2014915796

Printed in the United States
10 9 8 7 6 5 4 3 2 1

For more information or to contact the author, please go to
www.ForeverChangedBook.com
www.BreakingChainsInt.org

Author photograph: Potthast Studios

I would like to dedicate this book first and foremost to the Lord Jesus Christ. If it weren't for Him, and me seeing His goodness in the land of the living, I wouldn't be writing this book. I thank you for saving me and being with me all these years. Not only are You my God, You are my very Best Friend, my Husband, and everything I could ever want in my life. You are my life.

Next, I want to dedicate this book to my family and thank them for believing in me when I couldn't. This includes my mom and sister, who are in the cloud of witnesses cheering me on, my dad for putting up with me all these years, and my niece, Natalie, who encouraged me to keep writing and who has always seen me as a hero, even when I was at my worst. Natalie you are my hero now!

Contents

Acknowledgments

I want to thank Pastor Reggie and Bea Scarborough, as well as my church family, who have prayed me through this new adventure. Thank you, God, for Family Worship Center. What an awesome church! Also, I want to thank Denver and Sally Kemp. Even though we have the same last name, we aren't blood family. But, spiritually, we are closer. Thank you for the use of your cabin and just believing in me.

Thank you to Carol Lewis, Mary Thomas, Matthew Loomis, Sheena Kendrick, Vicki Durden, Sherry Embry, and Nicole Welch for their hard work in editing and encouraging me to keep writing.

I want to thank Chaplain Westmoreland and honor her by saying thank you so much for giving me Jesus. And for all the chaplains who are out there, don't get weary in teaching the Word of God to prisoners. Don't give up and don't quit. If it's just one life you save for Jesus, then it's worth it all.

Last but not least, thank you to all my other family and friends who have believed in me, encouraged me to keep going, corrected me when needed, cried with me, laughed with me, and gone on great adventures with me. Bless you all so much, and thank you for loving me when I couldn't love myself.

Introduction

A bruised reed He will not break, and a dimly burning wick He will not quench.

(Isaiah 42:3, ASV)

I would have never understood that statement if I had not experienced it myself. I was a smoldering wick on a candle, a bruised reed. Jesus was sent to heal the broken-hearted. A broken-hearted person is not just someone who has a hurt in his or her heart; no, a person that is broken-hearted is one who has been broken deeply inside and doesn't know how to function or even handle life as life is. Think about it. The symbol for a broken heart is a heart cracked down the middle, in two halves. I was broken in two halves. I remember that my mother and my sister would say, "The problem with Teresa is, she just doesn't know how to live." They were right, I didn't. I was broken like Humpty Dumpty, who took a great fall, but no king's horses came to put me back together again.

No child dreams of growing up and becoming a drug addict, an alcoholic, or an inmate in a state or federal prison. I have never heard of a child going to a parent and saying that when they grow up, they want to go to prison, or have their life ruined and ruin the lives of others. When I was a little girl in Indiana, I dreamed of being a doctor and doing great things to help people. Even in all my hurt and brokenness, I still dreamed of one day doing great things to change the world. So how does a little girl who dreamed of being a doctor become an ex-convict?

I remember seeing the deep pain in my mother's eyes, as she looked at her little girl in a blue uniform with big white letters that said,

"Seminole County Jail." I will never forget the end of our conversation on a phone with a thick glass separating us. As we said goodbye, she hung up the phone and then looked deeply into my eyes and put her hand to the glass, trying to touch the daughter that she had not hugged for nearly six months. She was relieved that I was safe and not dead somewhere in a ditch, but eighteen years of seeing her daughter destroy herself had taken a toll on her life. As I left the visitation center, I asked myself how I got here. Was there any hope for someone like me, addicted to drugs and alcohol for eighteen years, broken, dead inside, angry, and completely lost? What happened, what caused this; why am I like this, and how do I get out of my dilemma?

This is the true story of how God took a nothing and is making me into a something. This is a story of how the King came and put me back together again. For me to write a story about me is the most absurd thing I could think of. Even though I am a college graduate with a bachelor's degree in psychology, I am the worst speller, let alone writer. Why would anyone want to read a story about me when there are so many other great people in this world who have something to say? Really, this story is not about me; it's about a Deliverer, about the King of Kings. This story is about how a person without hope can have hope. This is about how people in prison can become free. This book is also a plea for the moms, dads, sisters, and brothers of an addict to not give up hope. Because a smoldering candle and a bruised reed, He will not put out or break. This book is dedicated to The One who can change the impossible. His name is Jesus. He is my Stronghold and my Hope, He is the Hope for humanity, and without Him, life is meaningless: "Return to the stronghold [of security and prosperity], you prisoners of hope; even today do I declare that I will restore double your former prosperity to you" (Zechariah 9:12).

Chapter 1

Reflections

How do you begin to tell a story that seems so unreal now? I have been forever changed. When looking back, I have to ask myself if this is even the truth. If it weren't for mug shots, I would seriously question whether I simply had a bad dream about someone else. It has been over seventeen years since my last drug or drink, my last attempt to kill myself, and my last trip in the backseat of a cop car or riding on a prison bus to a new home known as an "institution" somewhere in Florida.

My life wasn't always like that. No child grows up with dreams of destroying her life with drugs, sex, alcohol, and prison. I don't remember a lot of my childhood. I remember sitting in front of an old black-and-white TV watching a certain commercial, and when it came on I would run to my hobby horse, jump on it, and begin to ride as fast as I could, but not actually going anywhere.

From what I've been told, I was a cute kid. I loved to eat, play, and pester my big sister. Since she was twelve years older than me, I was a big nuisance. I remember wetting my bed and then running over to her bed and jumping in it, awaking her suddenly. Boy, she sure did not like that! She would start screaming as loud as she could, "MOTHER!" I was the baby of the family with two siblings. I had a sister and a brother, both much older than me. When looking back at my baby picture, I can see I was loved dearly and my eyes had so much joy in them, but something terrible happened to that little girl that hurt her deeply.

Before continuing this story, it's important to understand what abuse is. Medical dictionaries define abuse as any action that intentionally harms or injures another person. There are several major types of abuse: physical, sexual, substance, elderly, and psychological abuse. As I discovered on the Bureau of Justice statistics website (http://www.bjs.gov), the U.S. Department of Justice estimates that one in six victims suffers sexual abuse and is under the age of twelve. Sexual abuse takes the form of rape where the will is overcome by force; by fear through threats, manipulation, weapons, or drugs; because of mental impairment, where the victim is incapable of rational judgment; or if the victim is not of legal age established for consent.

What happens to a child when someone violates the trust they so freely give? The child is injured, and like the broken heart I spoke about in my introduction, the heart is split into two halves. The more a person is abused, the more the dissociation and shame, and that little beautiful creation from God goes into hiding. I think the worst thing anyone can do is hurt an innocent child, either by exploitation or simply not giving them the love they so desperately deserve and need. A child is so precious to God. They are trusting, truthful, loving, and forgiving. They are what we wish we could be once we get older. Children are the perfect example of what God wants us to be.

Before I begin to tell my story of how a sweet little girl can grow up to be a bitter and rotten adult, I want to say two things.

First, I no longer blame the choices I made on what happened to me. I made a lot of bad decisions because of the brokenness from abuse.

Many people have been abused and become great men and women in society. I didn't choose that path until later in life, after meeting the Lord who has forever changed me.

Second, I forgive and release everyone who hurt me. If you are reading this book, and I have ever hurt you in anyway, I ask you with great respect and sincerity of heart to please forgive me. I wasn't my true self; I was dealing with things from a broken heart, from being half a person.

This is the best way I can describe it: take a multi-colored clay pot and smash it with a hammer. It breaks into many pieces, all sizes and all different shades. After completely breaking the pot into pieces, take those pieces and fill a bag. Shake the bag and move those pieces all around. Then each day, remove one piece of the pot. You never know what you are going to get: a big piece with no color, or a small piece with a lot of color. That was how I was, simply a bag of broken pieces. You just didn't know what you were going to get day to day.

I suspect the abuse started around the age of five and continued for about a year until my family moved to a different neighborhood. We lived in a middle-class suburb of Indianapolis. I can still picture the outside of the house: it was a white stone home with a big basement; a pole for reinforcement stood by the staircase. As a little girl, I would grab a hold of that pole and slide down it.

I was a kid who loved to play and have fun. Dancing, singing, and listening to music were my favorite pastimes. I also loved to "read," even before I actually learned how to do it. Taking an old pair of glasses with no lenses in the frames (and worn upside down on my face), I would pretend to read. We had a big backyard with a sandbox and a baseball field nearby where my dad spent time coaching Little League. A little stream trickled through from our property to our neighbors' property. They had, if I remember correctly, eight kids, maybe fewer.

The oldest was a boy around seventeen, and the youngest was a girl the same age as me, four or five. We would often play together. To this day, I don't know if her brother, the oldest boy, hurt her or not. I would say that the possibility is strong. A sexual predator doesn't care. He is after one thing, and one thing only.

I can't remember the first time. I just remember it was often that my friend's older brother would get me and do things we won't talk about in this book. It's called rape and molestation. It's a complete violation of a little child's trust and spirit as it violates and mutilates the very being of a child. That is what it is designed to do, to destroy the person inside that God created. Abuse in any form destroys the victim's inner self, destroys the little girl or boy inside. We all have a little child inside that somehow gets crushed or injured, and then we shut down, allowing no one to enter that place. We go into a protection mode, and it can only be opened again by an all-knowing God who can gently heal and restore what was so messed up from the abuse.

I think it's important to explain what happens when a child is abused, whether sexually, verbally, or physically. What I discovered in my healing process is that the sexual abuse destroys the person inside that God created. We do have an enemy that is out to kill, steal, and destroy, but Jesus said He came to give us life so that we may live more abundantly. If you read the Bible and if you know the story of Adam and Eve at all, you know that when they sinned against God, they immediately went into hiding because of their shame.

When an individual is victimized through sexual abuse, the first thing they do is feel shame. Victims of abuse still feel shame even when they were not at fault. Unfortunately, that shame is toxic; it can destroy self-esteem and one's self-image. God wants us to love ourselves in a balanced way. After all, He made us, and He doesn't make mistakes; He said in the beginning of creation that what He created was good. We are created in His image, and therefore, we are His masterpiece, a work of art, made by the best Artist ever. Think about it. In the real world, thieves try to steal a valuable piece of art. They would never try to steal worthless art, like painting-by-numbers pieces. The enemy of our soul is doing just that. He wants to take the masterpiece God created and steal it for his purpose and for his plans, for evil and not good.

The definition of shame in the Merriam-Webster dictionary is "painful emotion caused by a consciousness of guilt, shortcoming, or impropriety." The Free Dictionary online defines shame as, "a painful emotion caused by a strong sense of guilt, embarrassment, unworthiness, or disgrace," and "one that brings dishonor, disgrace, or condemnation." The Bible makes it clear that there is a shame we ought to have and a shame we ought not to have. I heard one scholar call it, "misplaced shame" and "well-placed shame." The misplaced shame is shame that is not your fault, but was placed on you by others. As for the well-placed shame, there is a time we should feel ashamed for choices we make. Think how bad the world would be if people didn't have a conscience. They would never feel bad about anything they do. That is a person with a reprobate mind, and that person is dangerous.

When I was abused, misplaced shame is what happened to me. It created a shamed-based nature or personality. Someone else places this type of shame on you, and it thrives in negativity. The side effects of this type of shame are feelings of dishonor, embarrassment, awkwardness, and confusion. Misplaced shame is when someone else says or does something to us that make us feel like we are bad, not just that what we have done is bad, but that we *are* bad. Shame, guilt, and fear-based personalities lead to feelings of loss. Misplaced shame is the inner experience of not being wanted. It's feeling worthless, rejected, and cast-out. You pick up feelings of inadequacy and unworthiness, and this shame will make you detach from divine intervention.

Misplaced shame is not the same as guilt. With guilt there is a belief that one has done something bad. Someone with shame believes that she is bad, and because of this, feels un-loved because she is not loveable. Being shamed is the worst possible thing that can happen, because it conveys that one is not fit to live. Those shamed as children feel vulnerable, fear exposure, and have feelings of inferiority. Those adults don't believe they make mistakes. Instead, they believe they *are* a mistake. Shame-based individuals fear intimacy and avoid real commitment in relationships, and even though they may be in a crowd of people and with family members who love them, they still suffer from severe loneliness and isolation.

I remember experiences when the devil put misplaced shame on me. For instance, one day I was pushed from a bedroom window after my friend's older brother was finished with me because his mom came home unexpectedly. I was only four or five years old, so not only did I feel dirty, but also I felt like discarded trash. I remember how bad it hurt hitting the ground after being pushed from his bedroom window. I was crying, but I couldn't say why, nor did I know how to tell anyone what this boy had just done to me. I really didn't understand back then, being so young, but I just knew it was wrong.

I also remember times that he would corner me in his family's bathroom and do unspeakable things. I hated playing hide and seek, because it seemed he was always around to grab me and pull me into the family car in his parents' garage to abuse me once again.

After a while, I didn't want to go outside or play with the kids next door because I was afraid. All this started the development of a shame-based personality, and it continued through the next years.

After the year of abuse, even though he thought no one knew what he was doing to me, it seems the children around the neighborhood who played with us began to realize the dirty secret between us. When I got older, I wondered why I didn't tell anyone.

I would torment myself with self-reproaching questions, like, "Did I not say anything because I liked what was happening?" or, "Was I afraid?" or, "Was it a combination of the two?" I had to keep telling myself that I was only five. I was a child, not an adult; it was not my fault.

The day the abuse ended should have been a huge relief to me, but it only reinforced the shame I felt. I should have been protected and loved, but in my eyes, that is not what happened. The day was like any other day, children playing, my mom cooking dinner, my sister fighting with my mom about clothes and not being able to go shopping, my brother coming in from school, and my dad coming home from work. I had stopped riding my hobbyhorse, which now sat in the corner. I found a new place to hide myself: a child's beach lounge chair, the old kind with reinforced webbed nylon attached to an aluminum frame.

On this particular day, the older kids of the neighborhood must have felt it was their duty to come and tell my mom and dad what was happening. Unfortunately, they didn't do it with a compassionate heart, nor did they understand the extreme hurt they caused when they came to our front door.

We were all sitting at the dinner table when there was a knock on the door. I remember my dad was a little irritated for the interruption as my mom went to answer. Mom was ready to tell them that I could not come out and play when one of the older girls loudly stated that I was doing bad things with the neighbor boy and that my mom needed to know that her daughter was going along with it. Even as a five-year-old, I remember the shame and embarrassment that swept over me, and also the fear of not knowing what would happen next.

Despite the fact that what the girl at the front door was revealing was in no way my fault, having the secret exposed in front of my entire family was horrifying. My brother and sister were at the table, my mom at the front door, and my dad sitting at the head of the table. Also, there were at least four kids at the front door.

I ran from the table and went to the safest place I had at that time, my little beach chair. To this day, I can still remember how bad I felt. Along with the shame that the neighbor boy had placed on me with the sexual abuse, now more was placed on me by these kids telling my family just how bad I was. Not that something bad was happening to me, but that I was bad, not the boy who was hurting me, but me.

At that moment, and throughout my life until now, I felt that I never actually belonged anywhere. I became an outcast to my family and had trouble with all relationships from that point forward. It's amazing for me to look back now, in all my relationships and even being around a lot of people, I was always lonely and never, ever felt connected to anyone.

The shame that was placed on me from the abuse and how this abuse was reported permeated my very soul, and that was the beginning of my isolation and fears of intimacy. I was bad, and all fingers were pointed at me. As I ran to my little chair, my hiding place, tears ran down my face. Fear of punishment, embarrassment, and a host of other emotions ran through me.

Throughout the sexual abuse, I knew that what he, my friend's brother, was doing to me was wrong. I still don't know why I didn't tell my mom. Maybe I was afraid I was going to get into trouble. After all, wasn't it my fault that all this was happening? That is another thing shame will do to you: it makes you take responsibility for things that you have not done.

As I sat in my chair, I was alone and afraid. I remember my dad yelling something, so I thought for sure I was in trouble now. Yet, he never stopped eating after hearing the news; he never came across as protecting his little girl. At least that was how I saw it. That was what was etched in my little heart. Was I not good enough to be loved by him?

Suddenly, my mother came to the chair, grabbed my hand, pulled me up, and took me outside. She was taking me to the neighbor's house. I didn't want to go, but I was pulled along by her.

She entered their house and told my abuser's mom what the neighborhood kids had said. As I stood there listening, I felt numb. I hung my head in shame. The mother called her seventeen-year-old son. He stood silently. My mom asked him if he had ever hurt me. He said no. My mother looked at me and then looked back to him. She asked again, and he jokingly said, "I just kissed her once, the rest is not true." The verdict was in: *I was at fault. I was the guilty one.*

From that day on, I felt that I was guilty beyond a shadow of doubt. I was to blame, and I made up everything. He was innocent, and I was guilty. That was the end of it. There was no more discussion of it. Not long after that, we moved. To this day, I don't know if we moved because of the abuse or because of my dad's dream of living by a lake. The bottom line was, we never confronted the abuse. The damage was done, the hurt remained, and now there was a lot the devil could work with in this broken and abused child.

As I grew older, my mom took me back to the neighbor's house. I never knew why she did that. She was a friend with the mother of the boy who hurt me. In her defense, I guess she didn't really think that I remembered, or she didn't realize the seriousness of the abuse.

Eventually, I found out that I wasn't the only one. He had abused other girls. This was not a comfort to me. It made me even angrier to know that no one had stopped him and that he continued to make others suffer. I sometimes wonder where those victims are now and how they are processing the trauma; did they end up behind bars like I did?

I have to defend my parents, as they are good people. I am sure they didn't know what to do. In my little girl eyes, they didn't do a good job of protecting me. That was what I perceived, and that was reinforced throughout the rest of my life. I felt that I was not wanted, that I was bad, that my family was ashamed of me. But in their defense, they have loved me to the best of their ability; they are not to blame. Actually they did try to protect me, moving from their suburban home and away from their friends in order to get me away from my abuser, but I could not see it at the time. Also, this all happened in the 1960s, and at that time people just didn't know what to do about reporting abusers. As a result, everything just got ignored and pushed aside as if it didn't happen.

In the Bible, Ephesians 6:12 states, "For we are not wrestling with flesh and blood [contending only with physical opponents], but against the despotisms, against the powers, against [the master spirits who are] the world rulers of this present darkness, against the spirit forces of wickedness in the heavenly (supernatural) sphere." For me, it is amazing how abuse can distort everything. It causes victims to see themselves and their situations through a distorted lens, so the rest of their lives are built upon half-truths, or no truth at all. It's like looking at life through the bottom of a glass soda bottle; you can't see things clearly. Mark Twain once wrote, "You cannot depend on your eyes when your imagination is out of focus." This is why the light of

God's Word must come, so that the precious Holy Spirit—the Spirit of Truth—can show you what is real and what are lies.

Before going on, please understand that we can remain victims our entire lives, or become victors. At the time of any abuse or attack, you are a victim, but after that moment, you have to choose if you will let that event dictate the rest of your life in a negative way. If so, you then become a victimizer of yourself, not a victim. In your quest for vengeance, you become like the abuser, just what the devil wants you to be.

By allowing God into our lives, we are released from that prison of hopelessness and despair that the enemy wants for us. Instead, we can forgive and release our pain to God and become advocates of hope.

Chapter 2

The Journey

It's amazing that I am writing this book. There are a lot of books out there, all filled with ideas and antidotes, that are fun to read. There are also a lot of self-help books on how you can change your life, which, by the way, can work for a while, but will never have a long-lasting effect.

Writing this book is simply another part of my journey. I don't have it all together. I'm still figuring things out. The last thing I want is for this to be a simple how-to book, like how to redo your kitchen, how to plant a garden, or how to remodel your bathroom. I don't want this book to be a collection of mere words, but words that will produce hope, love, and life.

I don't want to suggest in this book that I have found the keys to complete success. Actually, there is only one book that can claim that: the Bible, the Word of God. But, with the Word of God, you must let the Word work within you and through you. So many times people, me included, have applied the Word to their life through self-effort instead of allowing the Word to work within and through you by its own power. The Bible states:

For the Word that God speaks is alive and full of power
[making it active, operative, energizing, and effective];
it is sharper than any two-edged sword, penetrating to
the dividing line of the breath of life (soul) and [the
immortal] spirit, and of joints and marrow [of the
deepest parts of our nature], exposing and sifting and
analyzing and judging the very thoughts and purposes
of the heart.

(Hebrews 4:12)

I have a story to tell about the power of God's Word. My hope
is to make someone hungry for God and to experience the power of
the Holy Spirit as I did. It's one thing to hear about Jesus, but it's a
whole different story when you experience Him. One touch from
Jesus can change anyone or anything. I found in my life that I must
be desperate for God—like I was on that July day in 1997 when Jesus
touched me.

At the time, I was so tired of being me and exhausted with what I
had become. I had been arrested seven times, messed up on drugs and
alcohol, and involved in pornography and other sexual perversions. I
stole, lied, and manipulated others. No child dreams of growing up to
be the person I was. Telling my story is scary, yet I know that telling my
story is sharing God's love.

Recently, I heard about a lady who died of a heart attack. She used
drugs and alcohol her whole life. She had no friends and died alone.
She made no positive difference in anyone's life. She had no possessions
and passed away without knowing Jesus. She was cremated by the
state in which she lived. She had no one, and no one seemed to care
about her.

Why do I mention her? Because if my story will stop one person from ending up like that, it's worth the risk of exposing everything I used to be and revealing what I am now. I pray that telling my story will encourage you and move you to know that there is a God in heaven and that no matter what you are going through, He will help you if you let Him. He yearns for you to ask Him for that help. He is such a gentleman that He will not override your will, nor does He interfere with your life if you don't want Him to. When people pray for you, and you pray to Him, He hears those prayers. He heard my mother all those times that she cried out to Him to save her daughter from the pit of destruction.

This book is a testimony. According to Merriam-Webster's dictionary, a testimony is defined as "an outward sign" or "an open acknowledgement," as well as "a public profession of a religious experience." So this book is a public profession of my experience with a living, caring God who has forever changed my life. My experience with God has produced an outward sign for all men to see.

I know you might be wondering why I share so much from my past, but to understand your future, you must examine your past. If you don't understand where you have been, you will never understand where you are going. People study history partly to avoid making the same bad choices others made in the past, but history also tells us which choices have provided blessings and prosperity. If we don't learn from history, then we will continue to go around and around the same mountains. I use mountains in the plural form because, in my case, I have had a lot of mountains, some that I continued to circle.

I started using drugs at a young age. I tried pot and speed when I was sixteen, and then I started drinking. I soon began using harder drugs and even more alcohol. I will soon be fifty-two, and I didn't begin this new journey without drugs and alcohol until I was thirty-six years old. Over eighteen years of my life were wasted doing drugs. I didn't accomplish much during that time. Looking back on my life, I proceed with caution and depend completely on the Holy Spirit, who is the Spirit of Truth, to help me in writing about my past.

After the sexual abuse I experienced as a child, lies easily became a part of me. Before coming to the Lord, I lived a life of complete deception. There is nothing worse than being deceived. A deceived person believes the lies so much that the lies become truth. That was my life—built on a foundation of lies.

After giving my life to the Lord, He had to let what I built up, my personal house of cards, completely crumble. He had to tear down the lies so that He could then rebuild me on a whole new foundation—one that was built on the truth of His Word. I saw through eyes of pain, rejection, shame, hatred, and bitterness, so everything I saw was dark and suspicious.

By telling my story, I want to leave a lasting mark on the Earth before I die. I have left other and more devastating marks, now I want to leave a positive legacy of what I have become because of what the Lord has done in my life. I am far from perfect, but I know that each day, no matter how hard it is, I never think about putting a needle in my arm as I did before. I might cry and scream, but most days I laugh and experience great joy, because now I feel that I am forever changed. I did nothing. He did it all. I just keep searching to find Him and to understand His ways. Do I understand completely? No, and honestly, no one understands God. He is too large and too amazing to understand. I do know this: He is faithful, good, and kind, and He loves me in spite of myself. He loves me when I am not loveable. Has the journey been worth it? Yes!

I sometimes listen to a song by Rita Springer, "Worth It All," that goes:

> Now around every corner
> And up every mountain
> I'm not looking for crowns
> Or the water from fountains
> I'm desperate in seeking, frantically believing
> That the sight of Your face
> Is all that I need
> I will say to You,
> It's going to be worth it.

The older I get and the more I know about God, the more I realize how little I know. I am grateful that He takes the foolish things and the weak things of this world to confound the wise. That includes me, because I am weak and foolish.

Why would you want to be weak and foolish? Think about the size and scope of God; consider how He alone is Wisdom, and then compare yourself to that. So, am I weak? Yes. But in my weakness, His perfect strength makes me strong. It has been good for me to realize that I don't know anything, nor can I do anything without the Lord's help.

All I know is that I am no longer who I was. The things I thought were fun and cool are now neither fun nor cool to me. The shame I felt is not there, and the lack of forgiveness that was stored deep in my heart is gone. Do I understand how that changed? No. There is so much that I don't understand. I don't understand how the wind comes and goes, or why the sky is blue, or how huge the universe really is.

How and why He did this for me is beyond my comprehension. But, He did it and it is because He loves me and He loves you too. That is one thing I have figured out. He is love and He can't do anything but love.

I have also learned that true love takes on a lot of different forms, beyond sending flowers or the easily spoken words, "I Love You." Basically, love is action. Love is denial of self. Love can hurt badly, yet love is worth the risk. This is why He sent His Son into the world.

Was it a risk for God to send His Son into the world? Of course, we humans want our own way. Could we actually believe that someone would die for us? Why would someone be so crazy to do that? But, the thing about it is, He did. He took the risk because He is true love, and true love laid down His life for us. I am so grateful He did that, because otherwise I wouldn't be here at this point. The journey would have ended April 16, 1997, and I would be dead and in hell right now.

"OK, you might be saying, what is she talking about?" Later, I will explain about the journey I took into hell, a type of hell here on Earth that I created, full of drugs, sex, lies, abuse, and such sick things. Love rescued me, and there was no one else who could have done it. You see, love is patient and will wait for the one who is being pursued by Love.

Love is correcting, which a lot of people don't understand. If God is love then I can be anything or act anyway I want to, because Love will always understand and forgive me. That is true, He forgives and understands. He understands that we are flesh and weak and that our body is simply dust. But God, who is love, is also a God of justice. Knowledge of God's Word brings with it responsibility to be obedient to His Word. The issues of life come out of our heart. Keeping our heart pure and clean will allow the power of God to manifest in our flesh.

It wouldn't be right to let your child play in a street when they want to do that. In fact, most parents who do that would likely be arrested for child abuse. In this scenario, a good parent who loves that child will punish them for playing in the street when they know better. Is the punishment to harm that child? No. It is to correct that child. Love is correction, and if God didn't punish or correct His child, then He would not be love.

Growing up, I wasn't corrected by anyone very much. I do remember moving away from the city, away from my abuser, and settling in the country. This was a dream both my parents shared—to live on a lake, and that is what we did.

It was great. I had ice skating and sledding in the winter and water-skiing and swimming in the summer. The woods surrounding us were so amazing. My little hound dog, Prince, and I would spend hours trooping throughout those woods. I was very much a loner growing up. I didn't have too many friends around, so it was mainly Prince and me. The times I got punished by my parents were because I was gone for hours, hiding in the woods.

As the baby of the family, I was spoiled. I think my mom and dad tried to give back to me due to guilt for what happened and out of love. They loved me a lot, but I simply couldn't respond to that love in a healthy way because of what had happened to me. It went in but didn't stay; I could hear the words and see the actions, but I couldn't absorb the love or take it in.

Growing up as a child in Monroe County, Indiana, was good. I water-skied almost every day, and it seemed I was in the water all the time. Later, as I matured, getting caught skinny-dipping in the lake after lights out was a regular occurrence. One time I recall my dad turning the floodlights on when my friend and I were up on an inner tube completely naked. When those lights went on, my girlfriend and I dove into the water as fast as we could. It was not a good situation, and I knew some form of punishment was coming as the flood lights immediately turned off. I heard my father say, "Teresa Lynn Kemp, come up here now!" Whenever you hear your first, middle, and last name spoken by a parent, you know you are in trouble. I was grounded for the whole summer. No water-skiing or swimming. They might as well have shot me. I begged them to whip me, beat me, anything—just don't take away my water-skiing. Boy did it hurt to see my friends ski by while I sat on the dock. They would wave and yell, "Hi Teresa!" Oh, just shoot me and get it over with! To no avail, my begging for a beating didn't work, but a neighbor who skinny-dipped at night a lot, (apparently that was his bath time), saved me by convincing my dad that lots of people skinny-dipped at night and it wasn't such a terrible thing. He talked him into letting me at least go back to skiing. To say the least, I never skinny-dipped again—well, at least not around my parents' house.

I do remember a lot of fun times during this period, before drugs entered my life at age sixteen. What is amazing though is how I really never felt I belonged anywhere. There wasn't a group of kids that seemed to fit with me. I always felt alone. Even being with others, I always felt like an outsider. I wanted to be someone and make something of myself so badly, but it just seemed as though I would go so far and fail again.

I actually began to even question if I was adopted, which I now know was due to feelings of inadequacy and inferiority. I didn't really feel welcome in my own family. I questioned any kind of affection shown to me. I didn't know how to love or be loved. If I did have friends, they were more like captives or hostages. I clung to them as a drowning person would a lifejacket or some other floatation device. I was like a dried up sponge encountering a drop of water. The water doesn't have a chance. It gets consumed by that sponge—thirsty for love and acceptance.

Throughout this book, I will be sharing my past extensively to paint a clearer picture of just how messed up I really was. This is so you will be able to grasp how God's miracle working power can change anyone, no matter how far they have drifted into darkness. I can't show how much of a miracle I am if I don't explain how badly I was in need of a miracle. It's the same way with people. If they don't see they are in need of a Savior, and, hopefully, someone reading this book will see that, then they will continue in their sin and go through life missing out on an awesome experience as being a friend of God.

During the abuse and immediately after it, things started changing with me. I gained a lot of weight. I ate constantly and also became more boyish. I didn't like being a girl. I honestly wanted to be a boy. I know now that I was in protection mode.

I started acting out at a young age. Even after we moved away from my abuser, I did things I was taught during the abuse. The sexual abuse aroused things in me that were not to be aroused at such a young age. As other boys came on the scene, I tried to smoke reeds at this young age and even got caught smoking cigarettes in the third grade. I stole cigarettes from my grandfather and from a little country store by my school. Sadly, my days of being a happy little girl were already over.

Being overweight didn't help matters. This made me more susceptible to additional hurt and abuse. Because of my obesity, my choice of wardrobe was limited. So I dressed sloppily, which reflected my inner feelings. I felt ugly and unwanted.

Proverbs 23:7 tells us, "For as he thinks in his heart, so is he." This is so true. How you see yourself on the inside will reflect your outside. I have noticed something just recently in my life. It sounds crazy, but when I started writing this book, I began looking back on the pain I had suffered and the misery I have caused others. Then, I started gaining weight. This was a reflection of what was going on inside of me. I ran to the refrigerator and ran away from divine intervention. That is a type of misplaced shame. Thank God for the precious Holy Spirit to help us see the truth. Thanks to God, I am back on track again.

Aside from the frequent lake activities, I don't remember much after we moved. There is a time period from about age five to age nine or ten that is somewhat a blur, like it never even happened.

The third grade is when I started to understand what had happened to me as a child. I went to a country school during this time. Now, when I say "country" school, that's what I mean—*country*! The only three things this town has are a post office, a country store, and a school. That was about it.

In third grade, we saw a movie about the birds and the bees. It wasn't graphic, but it covered topics like how a girl begins her menstrual period and what happens to a boy entering puberty. I don't know how to explain what happened to me, but seeing this film caused me to realize that something terrible had occurred. It was like all my past abuse that had stayed quietly dormant, silent in the dark on my insides, rose to the surface. I started having images in my memory from the sexual abuse. This made me angry at my parents, angry at the world, angry with God, and extremely angry with myself.

In fact, my self-hatred was so deep-seated that I didn't realize I was on the brink of ruining everything in my path.

I propelled myself into every sport I could—basketball, volleyball, and softball. I wasn't good at any of them. I was simply trying everything I could to be a part of something. I also tried playing in the band and with the city orchestra, where I played the clarinet and oboe. All these things were great, but still nothing fixed what was broken inside. I never felt at home in any of these activities. I never felt I belonged anywhere.

Chapter 3

The Trap

In middle school, while I could hold my own on the sports teams, I wasn't athletically-gifted compared to other kids in the school. I wasn't that bad, but going from a small, rural country school a big-city high school with many students meant I was in a more competitive environment. As the talent level of everyone went up, I eventually faded from that scene.

I became a chameleon. I adapted to be whatever I needed to be to fit in and find my way. A chameleon is a reptile that changes color in order to express fear or aggression. Interestingly, the color change happens because of the layers of skin chameleons have. They develop a variety of colors, including yellow, blue, and white. I had so many layers built up and so many walls formed around me that I would change into whatever personality was needed for me to be accepted—trying to be someone else so I would belong. It was like I took pieces of personalities from other people; I would observe what other people liked and were attracted to, and then acted that way to be accepted. Just like a chameleon. I would change to whoever seemed to be the "right" person to be with whatever crowd that would accept me.

I even remember that these kids that I would play with sometimes told me about this revival they were having at their church and asked me if I wanted to come. I agreed to go with these girls and their mother to their little country church in the backwoods of Indiana. I don't remember what went on nor what was said. It struck me as a little weird because they had no musical instruments in the church. Instead they blew a little horn in the key you were supposed to sing in. Then, everyone would try to stay in key, which they couldn't do very well. I have never forgotten that experience in all these years because they didn't believe in music, and I loved music. I thought it strange that God wouldn't like music. Now I know that He created music. When we get to heaven, it will be filled with glorious sounds of worship. Music was one of my escapes. I would listen for hours with different records, singing and dreaming of one day doing something great. Well, at the end of the service, I remember that everyone went down front and got into this pool. Being the swimmer that I was, I joined in. I never understood what it was for, but they said my sins were washed away. Since I felt so dirty from the secret I was keeping inside, I went into the pool a lot. In fact, every night I went to the water to get baptized and would come home with wet clothes, until one night my mother said, "You are not going back to that church."

My mom was my Sunday school teacher when I was a child. I remember going to church when I was little. In fact, I would always try to go home with my grandmother after church because there were always goodies to eat, and I loved my grandpa and grandma so much. My mom would tell me not to ask my grandmother if I could go home with her. So, instead of asking her, I would slide over very close to her in the pew, and then look up with desperation in my little puppy dog eyes. Staring intently at my grandmother, waiting for her to ask me, and without fail, she would. I would be at their house eating sweets and playing outside in the field behind their house. I knew about Jesus and heard the stories about Noah and the flood and all the animals, Jonah and the whale, and the others, but I didn't really know God. In fact, I was pretty angry with this so-called God who had failed me.

After beginning high school, sports had failed me, and music was not enjoyable anymore because the pressure of performance was too much for me. So, one of the colors that this chameleon took on was entering into the trap of drinking and experimenting with drugs. It's important that I explain that the addiction was not immediate. Abusing drugs over a period of time is how I got addicted. Also, drug addiction was a symptom to what was then going on inside me. It was much deeper than simple drug use. I knew that my abuse of alcohol and drugs was different because of the amount I would consume. I didn't do things halfway. It was all or nothing, and a compulsive and addictive behavior was manifesting itself.

Abusing drugs and addiction, even though they are sometimes used interchangeably, are two different things, very different conditions. "Drug abuse" refers to illegal or excessive drug use, deliberate use of an illegal drug or too much of a prescribed drug. On the other hand, "drug addiction," describes a disorder where the drug becomes The Boss. The drug becomes the dominant influence on a person's behavior. That person eats, sleeps, talks, and focuses on basically one thing, the drug of choice—The Boss. More specifically, when someone becomes addicted to drugs, that person becomes motivated and dominated by how to acquire the drug and then using that drug. All normality ceases. All normal constraints on the person's behavior are largely impacted. This addiction can be either physical or psychological. But, in either case, the only thought, focus, goal, and concern is where and how to obtain the drug—no matter the cost and no matter the consequences.

Not to get overly technical, but I think it is important to state that drug addiction statistics show that there is a growing trend of drug use, which will give us a window into the future. People need to hear the Good News of the gospel and the truth of God's Word, that there is a way out, that there is hope for someone who has fallen into the same trap I did.

My investigations on the website www.USNoDrugs.com—a comprehensive national directory of treatment centers and counseling services for those seeking treatment for addiction—have been enlightening. In one research study, I found that one in five people between the ages of sixteen and fifty-nine have abused drugs; they have taken some type of illegal drug. Statistics show that 19.5 million people over the age of twelve use illegal drugs in the United States, and that number has increased since the study from the Mayo Clinic. Over 19,000 deaths a year occur from drug addiction. This is an average of two deaths per hour, and that number is only reported from the Mayo Clinic's study. This figure does not include the homeless drug addict, which is usually not reported or cases where the cause of death is unknown. In the year 2000, there were over 600,000 estimated drug-related emergency room episodes, and the numbers have increased dramatically. Drugs and drug addiction are a cause for the increase in prison populations and crime. At this time, there are millions of men and women in the United States who are incarcerated as a result of some type of addiction.

Marijuana, or pot, was the first thing I tried. A lot of people ask me if it's true that pot will lead you to more dangerous drugs.

In my case, it did. This is primarily due to the kind of people who come with the pot-smoking. Pot introduces you to other people in the drug scene, which, in turn, introduces you to different drugs. This is what set the trap for me. Smoking pot made me feel different. I felt like I was invincible. As I desired to be different, I was. I think one of the biggest mistakes made about addiction and those who abuse drugs, is the assumption that those who are struggling under the drug's control are weak or somehow lack willpower and moral integrity. If you have a headache, you go get an aspirin to stop the pain. I was hurting, and I used drugs as my way of escape. Many people use food, sex, work, and all kinds of methods to avoid what they need to face. I didn't know how to face what was going on inside me, so I suppressed it. But, just like a pressure cooker, it will build a head of steam until you either let it out or it will blow up. In my case, I blew up. Gradually over eighteen years, the pressure increased until there was an explosion.

I was functional with pot and I liked speed. I didn't want to eat as much, and by the time I entered high school, my physical appearance had changed. I blossomed in the eighth grade, and, over the summer, I lost weight and I looked different. I started drinking and smoking cigarettes and then started hanging around the wrong crowd. I went back and forth. One moment I would be with a friend who was great at sports, very intelligent, and loved God, but then I would start hanging around party people. Eventually, the party people became more appealing. It became a slippery slope, and I started using stronger drugs like hallucinogens, AKA, acid, blotters, microdots, or "yellow sunshine." Hallucinogens are drugs that distort the way you perceive reality. They can cause you to see, feel, and hear things that don't exist—perfect for someone who was already having a problem with seeing reality and not coping with it. For me, the answer was to escape reality. So, further into the trap I went.

So many people when sharing a testimony lament or moan about their past, and not about the end result, which is, ultimately, victory over their struggles.

Truly, my story is a story of how the victim became a victor, and how a Healer came to heal the brokenhearted, the outcast and down-trodden individual that I was, without hope and with no life at all. Because of the Healer, I am now filled with hope and a bright future. As I mentioned earlier, for you to understand what a miracle I am, you must understand how deep into a pit I fell, the depths of despair I entered, and how wide the path of destruction in my life.

Surprisingly enough, I finished high school and entered into my first year of college. I was still functional, but just barely. I was like the picture of the cat that is hanging onto a limb with its claws, and the caption over the cat's head says, "Hang in there, baby." I was hanging on for dear life. I was in denial. To simply avoid anything and everything at all costs—"Fake It 'Til You Make It" was my motto. I had good intentions entering college. I really thought I wanted to be a nurse, so I enrolled at the University of Indiana in Bloomington. My parents paid for it all. I remember my precious mother working at a sorority house as a housekeeper. She did that for me, trying to give me a better future, but I just didn't get it. After a year, I was kicked out of school for not making the grades I needed to continue my studies. It was at this time I am sure that my abuse of drugs turned into drug addiction.

I started doing a lot of acid and drinking—a lot of drinking. I remember my mother being in a panic and shouting for my dad after I had collapsed after being out all night doing drugs. Because it was acid,

I came home extremely high and then fainted. I fell out of a chair onto the floor. They knew something was wrong but just weren't able to put their finger on it. The deeper I fell into the trap, the more I began hiding and feeling ashamed of myself for what I was doing. I liked drugs, and then sometimes I didn't. But, I did them anyway. Actually, it was as if I was punishing myself in a way. I had developed such self-hatred that I remember drinking a whole bottle of rubbing alcohol while looking in the mirror at my parents' lake home, watching myself as I drank every bit of it. I became so ill after drinking the rubbing alcohol that I vomited for a while, but then I would go out again and start doing the same the next day.

You know it's amazing how with God we are changed by glory to glory or by faith to faith, but on the other end of the spectrum, when you serve the devil as I was doing, you go from shame unto shame, despair unto despair, death unto death. No wonder the Bible states that "the wages of sin is death." That's the trap—deeper and deeper into a pit and only by a divine intervention can that person be rescued from the pit.

My life was such a mess it's hard to know what to put into this book. There is so much to tell. I am thankful that God has taken my mess and turned it into a message and that my story will hopefully help many people, at least stop them—or you—from making the choices that I did in my life. Regret is one of the worst enemies of all. I have lived a life of regrets, but now that I am with the Lord I have purposed to not have regrets in my life. One of God's many gifts, and there are a lot with Him, is giving us a life without regrets: to know that you have done your best in life, you have done your best for Him, for people, and made a positive impact while here on this earth. I have wasted a lot of time. Even though this book is hard for me to write, I pray that it will have a lasting effect, a positive effect on people's lives, that they, through this book, can find the One who will forever change them also.

I know there are people reading this book who have gone through or are still going through worse things than I have. I know a girl whose dad used her at the age of thirteen to test his methamphetamines on by shooting his drugs into her arm intravenously. I have heard of so many horrific stories of rape, incest, and betrayal. But, when these victims reached out to Jesus, their lives were never the same. He healed their broken hearts as He did mine.

I think it is important to explain that when we are in the pit of sin and destruction, that is all we see. It's similar to being blind for the blind cannot see, nor can a deaf person hear. In the next chapter, I will share some of the awful choices I made. I did what a sinner does; I sinned. You might even get mad at me for the choices I made in my past. I can understand that completely, because I lived with many regrets, shame, disgust, and simply anger with myself.

Even after coming to the Lord and giving my life to Him, I can't tell you how many years I lived in unforgiveness and self-anger. That is over now; it is a waste of time to do that. The sole purpose of Christ coming and dying on the cross was to take our sins. I'll let Him have the whole lot of them. How glorious that what I used to be I am not and that He, through no help from me, took all my sins and washed them away. Now, I won't give the devil the satisfaction of being mad at myself or others. The devil is a stupid jerk.

I heard one of the best analogies of how sin works in our lives. There are people who think that some sinners are worse than others, but that is not what the Word of God states. He said that we "all have sinned, and come short of the glory of God"; all have sinned. Maybe you might have not sinned to the degree that I did, but the Bible also says those who have been forgiven much, love much.

As I was praying this morning, I was asking the Lord, "How can I express the love I have for you in words?"

It is way over my head—it's almost indescribable the love I have for Him. Why? Because of how He reached down and got me out of the pit I was in. No matter how deep a valley in which you find yourself, the point is without Jesus we are *all* in a pit. Even if you are in the penthouse, if you don't know the Lord Jesus you are in a pit of sin, and you need to be rescued. If you take a power line and cut it, you lose power. If you keep cutting that power line, you don't keep losing power because that connection has already been broken. It takes a lineman to come and hook up the power line again. Jesus is the "lineman" who gives you a whole new line, not one that has been patched and held together by electrical tape. No, He gives you a whole new life. You become new on the inside.

I want this book to be a "life song" to Him. What do I mean by this? This book is the best way I can say thank you to the One who has forever changed me.

If He asked me if I wanted to start my life over again, have another chance and change my past, I think I would say no. Because I would be afraid that I would not know Him as I do now. Sometimes I feel sorry for people who haven't really gone through much trouble in life. People who have been saved their whole lives sometimes miss out on knowing God intimately. More to the point, they sometimes take Him for granted. But when you have been in a terrible pit and have had only darkness around you, and that arm of the Lord reaches down to get you when you least deserve it, it just makes you love Him even more. I pray you continue to read this book so that you will be hungry to know the

Lord even more and come to the knowledge, a deep knowledge, of His great love, compassion, mercy, and grace. He is not what the world says about Him. He is not mean or angry with you. He loves you and wants to help you, if you will let Him. Jesus came to save the sinner's heart, and His arm is not too short to save. He came not "to condemn the world, but to save the world." He came for the sick, the hurting, the drug addict, and the prostitute. He came to seek and save all those who are lost.

Chapter 4

Grave Clothes

There is a story in the Bible, in the book of John, which speaks of a man wearing "grave clothes." Grave clothes were essentially sheets of cloth that were wrapped around a dead body before it was placed into a grave.

The man wearing the grave clothes in this story was named Lazarus. As he had been in the grave for four days, he smelled bad. In my own life, I was digging a grave. Each year of abusing drugs and abusing myself, I continued to put more and more layers of grave clothes on. The choices I made produced a kind of death in me. Every abusive choice I made was producing death in my life. I walked around with layers of grave clothes.

Back in the time of Lazarus's life, burial garments were extremely heavy. Each cloth wrapped around the dead body was meant to keep disease out of the community. To prevent the spreading of disease, each cloth was soaked in different spices and oils during the burial preparation process. The weight of the grave clothes wrapped around the body, like a mummy, weighed over one hundred pounds. My life of sin worked the same way. Each bad choice I made put more weight on me, which produced more bondage, and more bondage produced less movement until I eventually died inside.

After moving from my parent's home and going out on my own, things deteriorated further. My mother and sister used to say, "The problem with Teresa is she just doesn't know how to live life." They were right.

My inability to handle anything in life was due to my heart being broken in half. I had no idea what I was doing. I wanted to do right, but I didn't really have the capacity to know what "right" looked like. My parents taught me what was right and wrong; I just didn't care.

By this time, I had lost some good friends and gained some bad friends. These negative, new friends in my life influenced me to go even further in the wrong direction. I wonder now who had the greatest influence, me or them?

You feel better when you hang around people who are just as messed up or worse than you are. I continued down my path of drinking and partying. I really began thinking that everyone in the world partied. I was high most of the time, even at work. I had a boss who was a pothead and would leave me a joint in the cash register. I would take the joint into the cooler at the convenience store where I worked and smoke it while on duty.

Before long I became extremely sexually active, which put on additional layers of grave clothes. Being abused had caused me to have a gamut of malfunctions in my emotions and behavior. Mark Twain said, "You cannot depend on your eyes when your imagination is out of focus." That was me.

I saw life and circumstances through the bottom of a soda bottle. Everything I saw and everything I felt was distorted by the abuse I suffered as a child. In my thoughts, having sexual relationships was the way to show love or how love was shown to me.

I craved attention. Positive or negative, it didn't matter. I allowed men and, yes, sometimes women, to use me, and I would use them. This lifestyle was detrimental, and it just reinforced the lies that had already been placed into my soul. I was trash, not worth any respect, and was incapable of respecting myself. The more sexual relations I had, the more drinking and drugs I did.

One morning I woke up and was sick. I was very sick, which continued for days. I had no energy. I was depressed and couldn't stop vomiting. The smell of any food made me sick, and I isolated myself because I was so ashamed. The phone rang continually, but I wouldn't answer it. It was my mother trying to reach me. My mom knew something was wrong.

One day my mom came to the mobile home where I was living and broke in. That is when we found out I was pregnant. I felt so ashamed of myself, and what I had become. But, I didn't know how to change or fix the problem. My mom worried about my baby because of my drinking and drugging, but she was also worried about me, her little Teresa. She wondered what would happen next.

My mother still had high hopes for me. She believed that one day I would straighten up and start caring about her, my life, and me in general. So at that point, we both decided that the best thing to do was to abort the child.

We were wrong. That was not the best thing to do, but people who walk in the dark inevitably trip and fall over the obstacles in their paths. It is only when you begin to walk in the light that you can see clearly and avoid the hurdles. To this day I am so sorry that I involved my mother in that terrible decision.

After I had an abortion, I fell even further into a pit of drugs and drinking. What was broken inside began a further process of obliteration. Obliteration is a strong word to use, but I looked up the meaning and the word best describes what happens to a person trapped in a downward spiral. *Obliteration* according to Dictionary.com means "destruction by annihilating something or the complete destruction of every trace of something." Used as a verb, *to obliterate*, according to the Merriam-Webster dictionary, means "to mark for deletion, rub off or erase." It also means "to remove completely from recognition or memory, do away with completely without leaving a trace."

That is the whole purpose of the enemy of our soul, Satan, to obliterate us or erase us from the picture. The Bible states: "The thief comes only in order to steal and kill and destroy. But I came that they may have and enjoy life, and have it in abundance (to the full, till it overflows)" (John 10:10). No wonder that in Ephesians 2:1 it states, "and you (He made alive), when you were dead by your trespasses and sins." That is exactly what sin does and is sent to do—obliterate the true person God has created you to be. Ever since the beginning of time, from Adam and Eve, sin entered into people's lives to destroy the spirit of God and their identity that is in Him.

Shortly after my first abortion, I got even more involved in drug use and was drinking quite heavily. I went from beer and wine to hard liquor. I started using cocaine, which I liked a lot. Many people feel that abortion is OK, but, I know from experience, it is not. It hurts the person emotionally, physically, and, especially, spiritually. Also it hurts the child, whether we want to admit it or not. Back then, I didn't understand that God made this child, just like I didn't understand that God made me. The pain from this abortion and others, even though I pushed down that pain, was great. I didn't understand the ramifications of my choices until now.

Honestly, it was as if another part of me had died, but the good news is that God is in the resurrection business.

Each time I put on more grave clothes, the deeper and heavier they became. Second Corinthians 2:16 states, "those who are perishing have an aroma, or savor of death unto death, it's a fatal odor, the smell of doom." In my life, I had a smell of doom.

Why do I share my story so candidly? I am surely not trying to glorify my past or the devil. I feel I need to show how deep into despair and sin I went so you can have hope that if God saved me, and He has, then He can save you.

I was the worst of the worst, but that is what is so glorious about the gospel of Jesus Christ. He made provision for the remission of my sins. Even before my parents had a thought of me, He thought of me. He knew what I was going to do. He knew the depths of the pit I was going to fall into, but He still chose to die for me anyway. That is a type of love that you don't find anywhere but in Him.

Isn't that what we are all looking for? To have someone love us in our mess and then love us enough to not let us stay there, but come and reach down, pull us out of our pit, and then seat us in high places with Him. In Psalms 18:4-6 tells us:

> The cords or bands of death surrounded me, and the streams of ungodliness and the torrents of ruin terrified me. The cords of Sheol (the place of the dead) surrounded me; the snares of death confronted and came upon me. In my distress (when seemingly closed in) I called upon the Lord and cried to my God; He heard my voice out of His temple, and my cry came before Him into His very ears.

Drugs make you do things you never dreamed you would do. You think that you are the boss of them, but in reality, you are out of control. Even though it seems that you have the upper hand. Everything I said I would never do, I did because of drugs. I made so many vows to myself, saying I wouldn't sleep around with men again, I would never steal, or lie, or manipulate, never have another abortion, would never go to jail or prison. The list of things I would "never do" went on and on. I am amazed that after what I went through I am still alive. If it weren't for my praying mom I wouldn't be here.

Listen to this. In I Corinthians 6:9-10, it states:

> Do you not know that the unrighteous and the wrong-doers will not inherit or have any share in the kingdom of God? Do not be deceived or misled: neither the impure and immoral, nor idolaters, nor adulterers, nor those who participate in homosexuality, nor cheats (swindlers and thieves), nor greedy graspers, nor drunkards, nor foul-mouthed revilers and slanderers, nor extortioners and robbers will inherit or have any share in the kingdom of God.

Because of the drug addiction, I became all of these things and then some.

If I had died before knowing Jesus, there would have been no hope for me. I attempted to take my life three times. On the last attempt, I ended up in a medical intensive care unit with black charcoal coming out of my nose and mouth because they had to pump my stomach. If I had died as I intended, I would be in hell right now.

Oh, to what depths pride and arrogance will take us. That last attempt on my life was close. I had purposed in my heart that I wouldn't wake up. I was at the house of a guy I knew. I decided I would attempt to kill myself by emptying his cabinet of downers and muscle relaxers, downing them with an entire bottle of gin. After all the pills and booze took effect on my body, I collapsed on his floor face down and was non-responsive. He drove me to the emergency room and dropped me off. If he had not done that, he would have woken up with a corpse in his living room.

Looking back, I am so thankful that he didn't just leave me on the floor. However, that guy was not so fortunate. He died of a drug overdose many years later.

After many years of abusing drugs and alcohol, I did try to clean myself up and make better choices. For about a year, I slowed down on partying and moved away to another city. Unfortunately, I moved with me. Moving away to another town helped for a short time, but it didn't solve the problem. I still drank, just less and not as often. That's when I began training to become a medical assistant. Surprisingly enough, I graduated and began a new career.

Since I was the problem and the issues inside had not been dealt with, I started doing drugs again, only this time more and more frequently. My parents moved away, and I moved back to the town I grew up in. I got involved with a married man who dealt drugs and loved to drink. So as you can imagine, I was off track again, wilder than ever. All those painful, dormant feelings came to the surface.

After a year of this, I was in bad shape. I just wanted to die. I was so ashamed of myself, of what I was doing and how I was acting. Every night people were over at my house partying. I woke up with terrible hangovers most mornings. Then, I would start drinking again despite the headache and queasy stomach. I had no respect for others or me, and I just wanted to end it all. But instead of attempting suicide, for some reason I chose to call my mom and dad in Florida and asked if she and dad would let me start over.

By this time, they had retired in Florida. They loved playing golf and having a reprieve from me, but drug addiction is like a cancer. It might seem like it is gone, but it comes back with a vengeance.

My parents did try hard to help me; they sent me to many counselors, but it didn't help. I was in church as a child, but after moving to the country we didn't attend church. God was not a source of conversation or help in our house until my situation got very bad. After moving to Florida, my mom went back to church and started praying.

They agreed for me to come and try another new start. At first, things were good. I got a good job working with cancer patients at a clinic located in Winter Haven. I loved helping people, and I was good at it. I purchased a car and things were looking up for me. I thought the move was it, and now both my parents and I thought that the hell I was causing was over and that I was going to make it.

Moving away is not usually the solution. Getting free and getting help from the Lord is the answer. At that time I wanted nothing to do with Him, unfortunately.

After I was there for about six months, I was asked to go have a drink at a pub located down the street from where I worked.

"It's OK. I can handle it," I told myself. And it was all right—for a while. I didn't go often, but it did get me out of the house. After all, I am no longer an alcoholic, right? I didn't have a drug or drinking problem. Months passed and I was still hanging in there. I still had my job and my car.

I started staying out later, a subtle yet ominous sign of things to come. I met some new friends and started spending a lot of time with them. This led to a return to smoking pot, and the drinking became a nightly affair, including the entire weekend.

Then one night after work, I walked into the bar that had become my hangout and sat down right beside a man I didn't know, who seemed nice enough. I quickly discovered he was a meth dealer in town.

That was the beginning of sorrows once again.

We started seeing each other and hanging out. I would finish work at five in the evening, spend all night in the bar, stay until last call for drinks or until closing time, and then get up early in the morning to go to work. Of course I'd be tired, so this new friend would give me large quantities of crystal ice or methamphetamines to give me energy. It looked like ice, and I would drop that in my coffee cup to keep me awake. That went on for a couple of years until I lost my job.

After losing my job, I did get hired a couple of more times thanks to the training and experience I had. I was trying to hold my own, even though I began smoking meth, snorting cocaine, and sometimes shooting cocaine in my veins. My facade of normalcy became increasingly difficult to maintain.

By this time, I had moved into an apartment with a friend, which was not a good situation. This "friendship" was a very sick relationship. There was a lot of co-dependency, we became involved with a lot of drugs together, and this opened the door to a lot of sexual perversion that continued for over eight years.

My life was rapidly decaying into complete destruction. I had lost all respect for everything. I drank every night, did drugs as much as I could afford, and just went down the tubes fast. At this point, my parents had watched me throw my life away for over thirteen years.

One time, my parents tried to get me help and put me in a rehab in Tampa. It worked while I was there, but after leaving the place, I went right back to drugs. My thought was, "Why do I need to go to all those meetings? I'm not an addict."

That's when my life collapsed into complete devastation. I could no longer stay with that friend. The friendship was so unhealthy that I mentally lost it. I was a mess. I was broken inside and everything from my past came gushing out. I was such a mess that it's hard to describe how bad I was.

I didn't have friends, but I held people like hostages. I clung to them as a drowning person clings to a floatation device, thinking I would die if I let them go. Not only was I involved in a perverted relationship, but I also became obsessed and idolized this person. It was like I got addicted to her, a perfect example of co-dependency. The relationship was so sick, but I was sick.

I was reaching for anything or anyone who could help me, but unfortunately for both of us, I reached into the pit of hell. I was looking for my identity in anything, but instead of looking higher and looking up, I went further into the downward spiral of addiction and what comes with it.

Homosexuality is the work of the flesh or the lower nature of our humanness. Homosexuality is a sin and a complete identity crisis. Just like idolatry, cheating, stealing, and fornication are sins. The fact is these sins scream "identity crisis!"

Drug addiction is also a sin and a symptom of a much bigger problem—a fallen nature, an identity crisis. With addiction comes all types of exposures to things that come straight from the pit of hell, including all types of pornography and perversions. The deeper I went, the less I cared and the more I lost my identity. The more I sinned, the more I died inside, until there was no life left.

When someone finally admits that they are gay, the world calls it "coming out." Actually, if you think about it, they are coming out. They are coming out of the original intent that God had planned for them. The Bible states, "That God created male and female, and that we were created in the image of God" (Genesis 1:27).

God is neither male nor female. He is a Spirit with three parts: Father, Son, and Holy Spirit. We are three parts also—spirit, soul, and body. We are a spirit first that lives in a body that has a soul. When we are born we are perfect, "untouched," so to speak, but because of the fallen nature of man, when the first man and woman, Adam and Eve, sinned, we inherited this junk in our souls.

God's first intent of man living in paradise was perfection, but thanks to the wrong choices made by Adam and Eve, we now live in an imperfect world. Adam sinned, and Eve was deceived. Adam knew, but Eve believed a lie, which is deception. That is what happened with me. I thought for the longest time that I was born with tendencies toward liking women, but that was deception. Looking back, I took the fruit, the lie, that was offered to me, just like Eve did. Why? Because I believed the lie over the truth and my lie became truth. That is deception. The sexual abuse introduced me to something wrong spiritually and physically. It opened up sexuality for me way before its time. I wasn't fully developed when the sexual abuse occurred, so I was easy prey to deception.

Looking back, I can see how I started to think that something was wrong with me. It started with mistrust of authority, especially male authority. Then I suffered with chronic suspicion and feelings of unworthiness that seeped into my soul. I began to get introduced to different sexual perversions that created more deception in my life to the point that I truly started to believe that God had made me the way I was. That is not true. For me, the more I hung around the gay scene, the more I thought I was gay. The more sexual perversion I was around, the more it became normal to me, just like the drugs. I thought everyone did drugs because all my "friends" were doing drugs.

What was happening to me was a complete "coming out" of what God truly created me to be. He created us to be like Him with His DNA. Sin genetically modified my spiritual DNA and changed me into someone else. When the truth of God's Word started working in my heart, I began to see what needed to be changed in me. I saw characteristics in me that were not consistent with God's character. I tried to change myself through outward changes like dressing differently, but that didn't work, that wasn't deep enough. I was still rough and tough on the inside.

My own walk with the Lord has shown me that it didn't take me overnight to get into the messed up shape I was in. It was years of sin that whittled away my original intent, which was looking and acting like God. Instead, I was whittled into everything that is "anti-God" and "pro-devil." I was genetically modified with his DNA. So this process of restoration was not going to happen overnight. What had to change was my heart—what was on the inside. When the inside changed then the outside naturally changed. Later in my story, you will see how God led me out of this identity crisis and helped me "come in" to my true identity and "come out" of the wrong identity.

In an article published in the February 1978 issue of *Christianity Today*, Bishop Bennett J. Sims said, "Sexuality and sexual behavior are dimensions of humanness, but they do not constitute a person as a human being." Our true identity is not based on sexuality or sexual behavior, nor is it based on what job we have or who our spouse is. Our true identity is not based on the car we drive or what kind of house we live in. Yet many people base their identity on these things, which is why so many people are devastated when a strong wind comes and blows the house down, or why businessmen during the Great Depression committed suicide after losing all their money. They felt their identity had been lost.

Our identity is in something that is greater than us. An all-knowing God who loves and cares for us and created us to be so much more than a lower, animalistic nature. He created us to be like Him, individuals with a higher nature that see things from an elevated perspective, from His perspective. Our true identity is that we are made in the image of God Almighty, and we have the great privilege of being a reflection of Him on this earth. If your identity is in anything besides Him, then you are in an acute state of an identity crisis. Worshipping the Creator instead of the creature solves our identity crisis. When we worship Him with our lives, we find our true identity.

God will bless us when we serve in His image. In essence, it is learning to come into agreement with God and not with this lower nature of ours. But, when we worship the creature, the self, the lower nature, we are then introducing ourselves to destructive behaviors. In doing so, we lose our identity as sons and daughters of God. We go from being God-conscious to self-conscious and fall into an agreement with the fallen nature, which gives us the characteristics and actions of the devil.

My mistaken or false identity was another form of grave clothes for me. It just added weight to my soul. Fortunately, God did not leave me in these heavy grave clothes. God showed me the truth that my identity was not in sex or relationships, drugs and drinking, or as a thief and robber, but my true identity was found in Him. The transformation was not immediate, but with the drugs, I needed a miracle right away, and Jesus gave it to me.

The issue of my true identity in Christ and my sexual identity was a process, a continuous conversion or transformation. When we come to the knowledge of Jesus Christ and allow the Spirit of God and His Word to start dictating our lives, things in our nature will change. I like to say, "When our insides change, then the outsides will follow." Our inward change will produce an outward sign.

God does miracles and He heals. One is quick and one you walk out with His guidance. The phrases, "Once an addict always an addict" and "Once you say you are gay you will always be that way," are absolutely not true! Jesus can do or change anything if you allow Him too.

When we live by the impulses of our natural state and let that rule over us, we are slaves to those impulses. We can lose our identity, the original state that God intended us to be. Colossians 2:9-10 (NEB) states, "It is in Christ that the complete being of the God-head dwells embodied, and in Him you have been brought to completion."

You will soon read the story of how God has and is bringing me to completion. Oh, if I can encourage you to keep reading, if I could place you inside me and let you feel as I do and see as I do now how God has touched my life. How wonderful it is to walk in the light of God and to see things from a heavenly perspective; there is nothing like it. God, help me to express how great it is to be a part of You, to have purpose now and to have truth. It is so wonderful to be different, to be like Him, and to let Him work in you daily, to be better and better. As you read further, you will see that receiving Jesus begins the process to becoming a new person. You will not be the same.

God's grace and Him working in you and through you are His process of renewal and restoration. You will become forever changed.

Chapter 5

The Line Was Crossed

Thirteen years of me being addicted to drugs took a heavy toll on my family. My mother would take me aside and say, "I don't like you. I love you, but don't like you." She wasn't alone. I didn't like me either.

Since I wasn't keeping any job, I lost several vehicles, and ultimately, I had to move back in with my parents. Still, during this time, I refused to admit that I had a problem.

To make matters worse, I was introduced to crack cocaine. I had smoked or freebased cocaine before, but crack is lethal. It didn't get a hold of me the first time I tried it. But, after a few times, I found myself meditating on my next hit. If I had any self-respect, crack and the spirit behind it was about to take the last ounce of any form of human dignity I possessed.

I remember the first time I went to the crack house. It's still vivid in my memory. I walked in and saw a girl sitting at the table. On that day, I walked in wearing a nursing uniform. I was working at the *hospital*—how scary is that?

That job would soon end. And so would life as I knew it. The girl looked at me after hitting on her pipe and told me to turn around and get out of there. She said, "You don't belong here and you don't want to start this stuff, because once you cross a line it's over."

I thought to myself, *You don't know who you are talking to. After all, I have it all together. I have been using drugs all this time, and I can handle it.*

She said again, "There is a line if you keep smoking crack that you will cross, and it is a line of no return. Once crossed, it will make you do things that you never dreamed you would do. It's like selling your soul to the devil."

I didn't listen, and I began using crack regularly. As I said earlier, things seemed OK at first. I was functioning, but that came to an end.

With crack cocaine you are always trying to chase your first high of the day. The first hit on the pipe literally makes you feel like your head is coming off. But, as an addict, this is what you are looking for, that euphoric-type feeling. The problem is you try over and over again to find that buzz but never accomplish it. It's like what the Bible states in a section of Haggai 1:6 in the *God's Word* translation: "You eat, but you're never full. You drink, but you're still thirsty, wine to drink but not enough to become drunk." You wear clothing, but you never have enough to keep you warm. You spend money as fast as you earn it."

This is a perfect description of how it is using crack. You chase that feeling of the first high, then live tormented because you never quite find it again. This causes you to do *anything* to get it.

One evening, I told my employer I didn't want to work for the hospital anymore. After that shift, I went straight to the crack house. The crack house was where I wanted to be. It was probably a good thing to no longer be at the hospital. That way, no one would get hurt from my incompetence. As I said the first couple of times, I thought I was OK. One evening at the crack house, I bought my dope and went into the bathroom, prepared my pipe and started hitting on it. On that day, while doing this, something happened. I remember it as plain as day—I crossed a line.

I saw life leave me as I looked in the mirror and took a hit on that pipe. It was as if my last few ounces of life drifted away and death took its place. It was as if something really bad got hold of me, and it did. I remember fear swept over me, even with the high I was getting. I remember feeling this terrible presence coming over me. I knew something serious had just happened, but like the girl I had met at the crack house said, there was no going back.

After reaching this point, I was not the same at all. I didn't care who I hurt or what I had to do. I was going to get high. I started staying away for days on end, and no one knew where I was. I lost all my friends who were not using drugs. The few I still had were no longer interested in me; I didn't care. The crack cocaine became my boss and I did what it told me to do.

I became so addicted to crack that I even walked through a tropical storm with torrential rains and winds. In Florida, there are hurricanes and tropical storms now and then. They produce great damage with winds that can exceed over a hundred miles per hour. I recall walking miles in this terrible storm, soaked and wet, but determined to get my dope, to reach the dope house.

I used to ask myself why, how did I get like this, why didn't I stop? Once I knew the Lord, He shared a verse with me in Hosea that explains this. In Hosea 4:11, it states, "Harlotry and wine and new wine take away the heart," or as the American King James Version phrases it, "Prostitution and wine and new wine take away the heart."

Think about that. Without your heart, you don't live. Your heart is the center of your very being. In Proverbs 4:23 we find, "Keep and guard your heart with all vigilance and above all that you guard, for out of it flow the springs of life."

Many athletes who train for sports or exercise work on what's called their "core." This is the area of the body that doesn't include legs and arms. The core of the athlete must be strengthened first. When the core is strong then the rest of the body will be strong, but if the core is weak then the rest of the body stays weak. Without a heart that is functional, we are weak.

I had lost everything. I used to say I would never sell myself for drugs, but I did that. I would walk the streets until I had blisters on my feet, trying to get enough money to buy my crack. Sometimes my frantic mom and dad would drive around the city to see if they could find me. I would jump in ditches and hide in toolsheds to keep them from finding me. One of the reasons I did that was my shame about the condition I was in. I did not want them to see me like that. But I also knew they would take me away from the one friend I had: crack.

I began stealing to support my habit. The arrests soon followed. After the first arrest, my parents put up a bond to get me out. They tried to get me involved in Alcoholics Anonymous (AA) and Narcotics Anonymous (NA), but to no avail. I lied and said I wouldn't do it again, but I knew in my heart that I was going back. I was coming to the end of my life but didn't know it. I was into my fifteenth year of drug addiction. I was truly addicted. I was past mere drug abuse. I was a full-blown addict.

The arrests started around 1993 or 1994 and continued until April 16, 1997. I was arrested seven times with no hope of making it. I didn't care anymore. One day, I was beat up with a vodka bottle. Drugged up and beat up, I went home and my mom begged my dad to help me. My dad had had it with me, and I don't blame him. I stole from them and simply couldn't be trusted. Any trace of their daughter was gone. I was wanted by the law, but I was in such bad shape my mother was afraid that if I went back to jail I would die. My mom and sister decided it was best to get me out of town. My mom put me on a bus with an assumed name and sent me to my sister house in Indiana so I could stay there for a while to see if that would help. When I got off the bus, my sister and my niece almost didn't recognize me. I was dirty and beat up, and it was obvious that I had been using drugs. It was heartbreaking for them to see the shape I was in.

My sister and her family went back to attending church, and my mom and dad starting going also. My mom was praying hard for me, along with the rest of the family. While I was staying at my sister's, her pastor came over to the house to talk with me. I received Jesus, and then he baptized me in the winter at a pond. I remember thinking, "Wow, hell is freezing over for me to get saved and baptized." There were actually snow geese on the pond that day. It was so cold, but I remember when I rose up out of that water, it was like all traces of crack cocaine—the taste and smell—came out of my mouth. It was amazing because even when I tried to get high from crack I couldn't—and I did try.

My time spent at my sister's had been good for me, both spiritually and physically, but my journey with drugs was not over yet. I said the words and repeated a prayer to receive Jesus, but there wasn't really a true repentance in my heart.

"By whatever anyone is made inferior or worse or is overcome, to that person or thing he is enslaved." This can be found in the Bible in II Peter 2:19. Verse 20 goes on to state, "For if, after they have escaped the pollutions of the world through the knowledge of our Lord and Savior Jesus Christ, they again become entangled in them and are overcome, their last condition is worse for them than the first." Verse 22 states in the same chapter, "The dog turns back to his own vomit, and the sow is washed only to wallow again in the mire." A strong statement, I know, but in my case it was true. My time of drug use wasn't over, and my last condition grew worse than my first.

I ended up going back to Florida. I turned myself in, and it wasn't long after being released that I went back to using drugs, this time even more, and I started shooting methamphetamines into my veins.

I went deeper into crime and doing more and more drugs. It was nothing for me to shoot up over five hundred dollars a day, some days more. I started stealing large amounts of money and using other people's credit cards. I had been arrested so many times that it became a joke, a routine. I remember that terrible sound when the cell doors closed. It sounds like death. It's a cold, steel-like sound. When they close you in and lock the door, the sound surges through your whole body. Being deloused, strip-searched, and fingerprinted became a norm for me.

Eighteen years of being addicted to drugs caused me to lose everything, and I developed an abased mind. "Abased" means to act in an undignified way, to behave in a way that lowers your sense of dignity or self-esteem. It literally means to bring to the base, or to the abyss, where I was. I was so deep in the pit that all lifelines were unreachable for me. There was no light left for me to see the lifelines being thrown my way. The drugs that were my friends had turned on me. I was truly a slave to them. So many days and nights I wanted to stop, but I kept doing them anyway. It was as if I had moved out of my body and the drugs had moved in. There is an old movie that I don't recall watching. I just remember the title: *Alice Doesn't Live Here Anymore.*

I identified with that. Teresa didn't live here anymore.

Eighteen years of drug addiction almost destroyed my family. Dad had completely disowned me. If it weren't for my mother, he would have cut me off a long time before. My mom just couldn't let go of her little girl, until one day I pushed her too hard.

I had all of Polk County's police officers looking for me thanks to sixteen different charges. I went from one place to another, hiding out in cheap hotels and shooting dope. I was like a cockroach. I only came out at night so I wouldn't be recognized. Sometimes I'd come out with a hat and glasses on so the police wouldn't spot me.

Things changed for me one day when I went home messed up on drugs and my mom knew that I was in trouble with the law again. The police had come by my parent's house looking for me.

My mother had reached her limit; I had moved out, Teresa wasn't her little girl anymore, and the drugs had moved in. I wasn't her daughter. I had become like a stranger and had been that way for a long time. Finally no longer able to take anymore, she had enough. She looked into my eyes and held up my baby picture in her hand. Her eyes filled with pain and sorrow, along with great anger. She tore that picture in half and told me that I was not welcome at her home ever again.

She looked into my eyes and said, "You are not my daughter, and you are not welcome here. My daughter is welcome, but you get out of here and don't return."

That was it for me; my last lifeline to any sense of civilization or anyone normal was now gone. The one person I thought I could continue using and depending on was cutting me off. Now the only thing I had left was my miserable self and drugs. Everything else was gone.

My mom and dad had given all they could give. As I said earlier, my dad had reached his limit much earlier with me. It's not that he didn't love me. Men are practical, and he knew that enabling me would eventually kill me. He and my mother had exhausted all avenues trying to help me.

There was now only one person remaining who could make a difference. I had to have a miracle or my life was over.

Seeing my mom tear up my baby picture was devastating. A great hole pierced my heart and soul. I truly felt like a person that not even a mother could love. My mom was my only friend who believed in me even after all I had done to her. Now, my rescuer had deserted me. I was alone; I had no one. My relationship with my mom was over; I didn't have any family left.

At least, that is what I thought. Sin is so selfish, particularly drug addiction; the addict is enslaved in a capsule of pride, self-centeredness, and denial. My mom had not rejected Teresa, her daughter. She had rejected the addict, the spirit behind the addict. Looking back now, I thank God that she came into agreement with my dad and decided she had had enough. When she did, it shook me to my very core.

My mother and father loved me enough that they stopped enabling the addiction in my life. The tough love they showed me is one of the things that saved my life. I don't even want to think about what would have happened if she had not torn my baby picture in half. What courage it took for her to do that. She really had no choice. She was losing me. Now, I know it was her last ditch effort to try to save her daughter. Mom knew it was time to cut me loose. That dramatic act of cutting me loose is what led me to getting help.

It was a painful risk for them, but it was a right risk. Because it caused the entire burden of the addiction to fall on my shoulders now. There would be no more bonding out, no more financial rescues, no more "help," because helping me only kept me an addict. It was up to me now. If I made bad choices, then I was going to be fully responsible for them.

What my mom and dad did by reaching their limit of helping me was true love. It's like the story in the Bible of the prodigal son, found in the fifteenth chapter of Luke. This son only wanted what the father had, the material goods, not a relationship with him. He had the selfish attitude of give me what I want. I don't care about you, just what you can give me.

I was just like that son. In the story, this particular son asked for his portion of the inheritance, then went out and wasted his whole life on riotous living. Like me, this son fell into a deep despair of famine and need. He fell to the bottom of the pit. What happens next saved that boy's life. The Bible states that he went and fixed himself upon a stranger. That's what I did. I left all I knew and became a slave to a stranger that made me eat with the pigs, just as this boy did. He left all the goodness of his father and family to dwell with the sows. Why? Whatever you become a slave to becomes your master. Like this young man, my master was riotous living. As this boy was starving to death, the Bible states he literally started to eat the food of the pigs. I ended up there too.

But while he wallowed in the pig dung, eating with the pigs, the Bible states "he came to himself." *He came to himself.*

Why do I share this story? Because when my mom and dad let me go, even though at the time I thought, *See all this time you didn't love me*, it was true. I pulled out my trump card by using the manipulation ploy of guilt. "Oh, what a poor victim I am," I cried!

Thank God those manipulation tactics didn't work anymore. They took a brave stand and stopped enabling me. Terrible hardships followed that loss of security. All I had known before was a life of security in the knowledge that no matter how I screwed up, my mom would always be there to rescue me from my mistakes. I was now alone, by myself and responsible for me. From that day forth those hardships were going to break me and bring a change. Those hardships were going to make me see that I was eating with pigs.

Enabling is not the same as helping. Enabling has two meanings: one is positive, while the latter is negative. The positive side of enabling refers to patterns of interaction that allow individuals to develop and grow. The negative meaning is what, unfortunately, happened to me for eighteen years. No fault to anyone, but people are destroyed for lack of knowledge and understanding.

With difficult, problematic behavior, the negative sense of enabling is used to signify dysfunctional approaches that are intended to help, but, in fact, may prolong a problem. Enabling is where third parties take responsibility or accept blame or make accommodations for a person's harmful conduct (often with the best intentions, like my parents), and with these best intentions come fear and insecurity. My parents feared losing me, or finding me dead in the ditch somewhere. They waited for the phone to ring, or for a police officer to come and tell them their daughter was dead. If I remember right, they actually purchased life insurance for me so they could afford to bury me properly. Every arrest brought relief to them because they knew I was safe and off drugs.

In any event, the practical effect of enabling is that the person being enabled does not have to take responsibility for their actions, is shielded from the awareness of the harm they do to others, and is spared any pressure to change. Here's one of my own simple definitions of enabling: when you enable an addict or anyone with a problem, you make it possible and easy for that individual to stay the same. To enable someone also gives the person who is causing harm to themselves and others permission or the right to continue to do it.

She Came to the End of Herself

I left the county I lived in. Considering there were sixteen charges hanging over my head, I thought it was best to get out of town. My mother told me that she and my dad didn't want to hear from me. They didn't want to know where I was because if they found out, they would tell the police. It was me, the drugs, and another girl who was just like me, on a journey. The law wanted her, like me, and to us it was a perfect situation. I borrowed a man's truck that I never returned to him. In other words, I stole his truck and left town.

We moved from town to town, until we decided to live in Daytona Beach. Day after day and night after night, it was the same things— drugs, drinking, stealing, and everything else that goes with that. We were renting a place right across from the ocean, and we would travel back and forth into Polk County at night to get our dope because we had not connected yet to drug dealers in Daytona. I had reached a new low. I was in so deep that I didn't care if I went further into the pit.

I would sometimes call my mom and dad's house just to hear one of their voices on the phone and then hang up. I was using more drugs now. I was shooting up so much meth that at times I would pass out after a big hit. I would fill my syringe up over and over again. Sleeping wasn't an option anymore. I recall one stretch where I stayed awake for twelve days with just a little hour here or there of sleep. My days were numbered and I had a sense of it now. The girl who was my partner in crime started telling me that I was going to kill myself with the amount of dope I was using. She would beg me to stop, but I wouldn't listen. I was already resolved to dying and going to hell. That was OK with me. As I said earlier, I was in such a pit that going to the pit simply didn't matter.

One day as I was driving down the beach at Daytona, I was struck with an immense sense of fear. So much fear that I could hardly breathe. I have never forgotten to this day the voice I heard, an audible voice, and what it said. My friend didn't hear it, but I did.

The voice said three things: "Your sister is going to die, you're going to prison, and your mom is going to die also!" I was in a panic, but instead of just stopping the madness I thought the best thing was to just use so much dope that it would not look like a suicide but a drug overdose. After all, everyone would expect that.

You could smell death on me that day. I could feel evil all around me, and now I know it was hell coming to get me. My partner in crime looked at me as I drove down the highway heading back to Daytona. She said, "Someone is dying today, and it's not me."

She was right. I even had a glove compartment full of syringes filled with meth. I had been up with no food or sleep for days. As I was driving I got confused, and instead of heading to Daytona I turned around and ended up going west instead of east. As I went off the highway and pulled into a gas station, a police car followed.

We were involved in a lot of identity theft, and I had used a lot of different names, so when the police officer got out of his car and asked for my license, I knew it was soon to be over. We were in a stolen truck, which he said had expired tags. But, I had stolen the tag that was on the truck, and I knew it wasn't expired. He also said he was pulling me over for not having a seatbelt on, but I was parked. When the officer asked me to get out of the car, I did, but I was a mess. He asked me what my name was, and with complete exhaustion I told him, "I don't know what my name is, maybe Margaret or maybe Teresa, I don't know." He told me to turn around, placed handcuffs on me, and arrested me on the spot. Since both my partner in crime and I had outstanding warrants in another county, our names were not revealed until much later.

We did not realize the police were following us because we were under investigation for the crimes we were committing. I thought someone was following us, but it was hard to tell if it was paranoia from the drug use and lack of sleep or if it was real. It *was* real. It's so amazing to me how deceived a person can become to even think that they can continue such a path of crime and not get caught. Thank God I did. The voice said that I would go to prison, and now it looked like that was about to happen.

I found out later that this was at the same time my mother had called my sister Jackie and told her and my niece to start praying for me. My mom knew something really awful was happening to me, even though it had been months since she had seen or heard from me. My mother told my sister to start praying, that she felt I was dying. My mom prayed, but my niece told me that she and my sister could not pray for me. They attempted over and over again to find the words to pray for me, but it was if the heavens had closed on me. They actually thought I was already dead.

On April 16, 1997, after being arrested seven times, my life was about to take a drastic turn. I was in the holding cell getting processed.

Before the detective started to question us, even though I acted upset that I was caught, I was relieved. I knew I was in big trouble, but I sighed with relief that I could rest now. I was so burned out and so tormented. The drugs that were my friends had become a big enemy to me. The jail cell would be my reprieve from the drugs' persistent nagging.

For the next two weeks, I didn't do anything but sleep. Some of the ladies in my cell tried to take care of me by bringing up some food or trying to wake me up to go down for chow. I had a lot of sleep to catch up on. My body was trying to recover. My partner in crime was in a different cell. We were at the Seminole County Jail in Sanford. I had no idea where we were or what was going on. My name at the time was Jane Doe because I couldn't tell them my name, nor did I want to.

I tried calling my parents to no avail. When they cut me off, they truly cut me off. But it was the best thing that could have ever happened to me. I finally had a chance to hit bottom, and with no rescuer there to get me out, I had to face it head-on or just die. Either way, it was on me this time—no one to blame except me.

It was about a month before I was functional. Even then, I was extremely paranoid and had facial tics caused from the drug use. I was coming off the drugs bad, not only drugs, but alcohol and cigarettes. I was not a happy camper.

I had deprived myself of food for so long that I would eat like an animal when they gave us food. If the other ladies in my cell had anything left on their plates, I would eat that also. I ate and slept, and that was my life. I ordered every sweet thing I could through the commissary with the money I had in my possession when I was arrested. I ate as much sugar as I could to help with my cravings for drugs. I am talking about boxes of Little Debbie's Oatmeal Cream pies. If I kept up this type of eating, before long, I was going to be as big as a house, and I would need a bigger uniform.

I tried for months, but my parents still wouldn't answer my phone calls. I was trying to figure out how my friend and I could get bonded out before they found out who we were. Since my friend and I were in different cells, the only options to be able to meet and talk with each other were GED classes, which I didn't need, and church, which I thought I didn't need either. I started going to church in jail, but I had no interest in God. I thought He had no interest in me. I just wanted to see my partner in crime and figure out how to get out of this place.

In June, they found out who we were and told me that I was in big trouble. Not only was Polk County going to come and get me, but I also had new charges in Seminole County, and the Federal officers came to see me for the mail theft crimes. Now, not only was I facing state charges, but I was also facing federal charges.

As the federal officer flashed his shiny gold badge at me, he identified himself and told me they had all the evidence they needed to prove my guilt. They had found our apartment at the beach; they had the computer—they had it all.

He looked straight into my eyes and said, "Lady, you are in a lot of trouble, and with all the charges you have against you, you will be gone for a long time. You, Miss Teresa Kemp, are looking at forty years for all these charges combined."

When he said that, I started to break. I didn't cry, but I started into this weird little laugh. I wasn't trying to disrespect him, but I was having something like a nervous breakdown. As they led me back to my cell I continued to laugh. That went on for a while. Then I cried and cried. I was going to prison and that was it, no way around it and no getting out. It was over; my life was *over*.

I continued to meet my partner in crime in the church. One day, we were talking while the chaplain of the jail was trying to preach. We were so disrespectful. She told us to be quiet. I thought to myself, *Who does she think she is, and what kind of Christian is she to tell me to be quiet?* We continued to misbehave and she told us to be quiet again but this time with even more authority, and she said that if we didn't quiet down, she would separate us. That did it for me. I said, "OK we will stop. Just don't separate us." At least we could trade notes and talk that way.

After we became quiet, I started to listen to what she was saying. She was talking about this man called Jesus. Of course, I had heard about Him before. But, honestly I had really stopped believing in anything. I was on the dark side. When you're lost and you are blinded to the truth, you can justify anything to make excuses for your wrongdoing. It's easier to say you don't believe than to change.

It was amazing what I was hearing. I heard that Jesus would forgive me and that He would wash away all my sins. When He died on the cross He thought of me. I thought to myself, *What a joke. How in the world could He forgive me? I broke every commandment in the Bible and then a few more.* But the more I listened, the more something was happening in my heart. I didn't know it, but I was about to have an encounter with God. Like the prodigal son when he came to himself, I was about to come to myself.

Chapter 7

He Reached Down

Therefore He is able also to save to the uttermost
(completely, perfectly, finally, and for all time and
eternity) those who come to God through Him.

(Hebrews 7:25)

It was July when they had moved my partner in crime into my pod. We still attended church, and I actually was listening even more. A church volunteer named Jan would come into my cell to do a Bible study. My friend liked her and would go down the stairs to listen to the teachings of Jesus. I, on the other hand, would stay in my cell, far away. I could still hear her teaching. Eventually, I moved from my cell to the railing on the second floor and looked over to watch her teach. Eventually, I moved closer and closer, first to the railing where I stood for a while, then closer to the stairs where I sat. Finally, I sat at the tables around her just listening.

One day I tried again to call my parents, and to my surprise my mom answered. She didn't sound right. I thought at first, it was because she was still really mad at me and didn't want to talk with me. But with her voice quivering she told me that my sister Jackie was dying. My heart sank to my feet. My sister was only forty-six years old. She had diabetes from childhood, and because of the complications caused by that disease, her organs were shutting down.

This brought back the memory of what happened before I ended up in jail. My sister had been sick for a while, so much so that I left Florida for a short time and went to take care of her in Indiana. I was still severely addicted, but I had managed to abstain from drug use (not alcohol, but drugs) while I was with her. My idea was to be with her and to help her, but I couldn't help much, because I was such a mess. A drowning person can't help someone else who is drowning as well.

I worked at a convenience store at night, in the small town where my sister lived. I made donuts at night, and then slept most of the day. My intentions were good. I did really love my sister. We would have so much fun together, and she believed in me, as my mom did. She, my mom, and my niece kept seeing the "real Teresa" instead of what the drugs had created. I think that is what parents of addicts do. They don't mean to enable their child to remain on drugs, but they know what is *in* their child. They believe in and love their child. They know that it's not really their child they are watching destroy their lives. So, as loving parents, they keep thinking and believing that maybe today will be the day that their child will see. With me, that day didn't come until I reached a deep bottom. Hearing about my sister sent me to the place of brokenness that would change me forever.

I stayed with my sister as long as I could, and that wasn't very long. Jackie was dying, but the only thing I could focus on was the drugs and on me. I had saved some money while being at her home and decided I would leave her and go back to Florida. I thought I would get high for about a week and then come back and be with her. That week turned into no return at all. Jackie begged me not to go. I remember her telling me, "If you leave me this time, you will never see me again." I told her that was not true and I would be back. I never came back to her. After leaving her, I had gone way off the deep end. She was right. I would never see her again.

Standing at that phone inside Seminole County Jail and hearing the words that my sister was dying sent complete anguish through me. My mom said that she and my dad would not be in Florida but were leaving to be with my sister. As I listened to the pain in my mom's voice and thought about Jackie begging me not to leave her, I, for the first time, started seeing what a jerk I had become.

This time there was nothing to numb the pain, no one to blame other than myself, and no denying what I had to see. Before, it was always as if I looked through the bottom of a Coke bottle to examine my life, I was in denial and living one big lie. It was always everyone else's fault. I was always able to justify my actions, because I was abused as a child. I had been mistreated. Now, the truth of who I was and what I had allowed the drugs and a life of complete selfishness to do to my family and me was staring me in the face, and it was ugly. Guilt, shame, the pain of losing my sister, and complete despair overwhelmed me. Not only was I in a prison cell in the real world; I was imprisoned in my mind with guilt and regrets. I felt such overwhelming shame and disgust about myself. It was unbearable.

I remember asking my mother if I could call again to Indiana to see what was happening with Jackie, and she agreed. I told my mom I loved her, but there was no response. She was so hurt. Not only was my mom losing her daughter, but also, she had another daughter looking at forty years in prison. I never thought about her and what pain she must have been going through.

I hung up the phone and went to my cell. It was then that I couldn't get away from me. It was then that I began to really examine my life. It didn't matter about the charges that I was facing. I didn't even think of them. I could only think about my sister, and I knew in my heart she was going to heaven. She had always loved Jesus. But I also knew that I was going to hell. I can't explain really in words the anguish that I felt.

Early in my story, I talked about well-placed shame and misplaced shame. Misplaced shame is shame that is not your fault, but was placed on you by others, like when you suffer sexual abuse. Well-placed shame is when we should feel ashamed about choices we make. What was happening to me was like a motion picture of my life playing before me. I began to see what I had become and how wrong I had been. I was facing truth for the first time in my life. I didn't like what I was seeing or what I had become, but it was the only thing that was going to help me. It was painful to have to see all the ugliness in me. I was imprisoned with thoughts of failure and deep levels of guilt and shame, so much so that I didn't know how to express the intensity of the many emotions engulfing me. Facing the truth was actually going to set me free and give me a whole new outlook on life. The Bible states that "the Truth will set you free" (John 8:32), and that Jesus is "the Way and the Truth and the Life" (John 14:6). And, I was about to meet Him.

I guess it was about a week that I had gone through what I now know was "Godly sorrow." The Bible explains Godly sorrow in II Corinthians 7:10-11. Godly sorrow was producing in me earnestness and an eagerness to clear myself. It brought about indignation and an alarm that I needed justice for my actions, for my sins. Little did I know I was having a "Godly grief," and it was producing a deep sadness in me that I was experiencing as a result of all the sins I had committed. That verse states in the *God's Word* translation, "In fact, to be distressed in a Godly way causes people to change the way they think and leads them to be saved. No one can regret that. But the distress that the world causes brings only death."

I was in such a pit and never realized how deep in the pit I was until I looked up to try to see some type of light, anything that would show a way out of that pit. I began to think about how there had to be another way than the way I had chosen. There had to be a way out of this, out of this pain. There had to be more to life than this. I didn't know how I had gotten like this, but I didn't want to live like this anymore. I had no hope. I had nothing but this one thought: *Maybe if I give my life over to this God they are talking about, maybe He could show me how to get out of this pit.*

I went to my friend and told her I didn't want to be like this anymore. I wanted to change, and the next time I went to church I was going to ask them to pray for me and do that thing they did, when they raised their hands and gave their life to Jesus. I thought to myself that I had missed out on being with my sister in this life, but if it was true about Jesus, that I would have eternal life with Him. I knew Jackie was going to be in heaven. I would ask Jesus into my heart so that I wouldn't be separated from her for eternity. Honestly, I wasn't getting saved to be with Jesus, but to be with Jackie.

That morning was different for me. Going to church, I didn't know what was going to happen. I just knew that this one time, I really wanted to go. The day was July 20, 1997, and it was about 9:30 a.m. I can't tell you what Chaplain Westmoreland said or what she preached. I only knew I couldn't wait until she was finished and asked if someone would like to receive Jesus as their Lord and Savior.

I had no idea what I was doing. I was hoping so desperately that it would be a lifeline for me out of this, what I was feeling, and if not, that at least I would be with Jackie again somehow. I remember it like it was yesterday. I can tell you where I was seated in the jail chapel and how gorgeous of a day it was outside. There was a window where I was sitting. I even remember the dew on the ground from the morning. When Chaplain Westmoreland asked if anyone wanted to receive Jesus, I raised my hand instantly and asked Him to forgive me of all my sins, for everything I had done, and then to come into my heart. I then made Him my Lord and Savior.

I was different from that day forward. Something happened to me. I could feel I was different. I wasn't so heavy anymore with the weight of feeling so bad about myself. I still felt bad, but I could feel hope. When I went back to my cell, I didn't want to fight or cuss or even play cards. I just wanted to get a Bible and start reading it. I wanted to know what had just happened to me, because I could tell that I wasn't the same. I was happy, and I hadn't felt that in a long time. I couldn't wait to call my mom and my sister to tell them that I had just given my life to the Lord.

When I called and told my mom, she was hurting so much she couldn't really grasp what had happened to me. Plus, I had lied and put her through so much, she didn't know what to believe. It was OK for me, because I could tell something had happened. I didn't know what yet, but something had changed. I didn't feel I was in prison anymore. I felt free and relieved. There was life in me, and I hadn't felt that in a long time. I knew I had never felt this way before in my entire life.

I asked my mom if I could speak with my sister, and she told me she was on her deathbed and couldn't talk to me. So I asked my mother to please hold the phone to my sister's ear so I could tell her what had just happened to me. My mom did, and I spoke into the phone, "Jackie, I am so sorry for what I did. Please forgive me. I love you, and today I gave my life to Jesus. I might have left you in this life, but I am saved now, so I will be with you in the next life!"

I didn't hear any response, but I believe she heard it. My mom took the phone away from her ear, and then I told my mom I was sorry and asked her to forgive me also for all the pain I had caused her and that I was sorry for not being there for her and Jackie. Then, the conversation was over. I was saved on the 20th of July. My sister died three days later on the 23rd. It was her death that brought me life, but more importantly, it was Jesus's death that brought both of us life.

The day my sister died, I was called to the chaplain's office in the jail. The church lady, Jan, who did the Bible studies in our cell, was there with the other chaplain who I didn't know very well. They graciously told me about my sister and prayed for me. Then they told me that they were going to move me into another cell. I was so hurt inside that there wasn't one place on my body that didn't hurt. The emotional pain was so great that it made my body ache. It was a complete brokenness. Now in addition to hearing about the death of my sister, they were going to move me away from my partner in crime. She had gotten saved the same day as I did, and I didn't want to be separated from her, not now. I wanted her to help me through the pain I was experiencing. Looking back, I thank God that those women did what the Lord told them to do.

After returning to my cell, I was completely broken and lost, I was numb. They came and got me from my pod and moved me across the hall into a Christian dorm, or a faith-based dorm. There were no beds; it was overcrowded. I actually was sleeping on the floor between the toilet and a wall. My feet were right by the toilet, but they had wanted me moved as quickly as possible. If someone used the toilet after lock down, I would have to turn my back and, at times, hold my breath until that embarrassing moment was over.

I was not happy, and as the steal metal door closed I screamed, "No, I don't want to be here!"

It was too late; the door was shut and there was no escape. Mind you, I didn't know Jesus. I just had gotten saved, but I still didn't understand what that entailed or what He had changed in me. I was completely unaware of salvation and the new birth. I was ready for a change but not one so drastic, and especially not at this time. I had just been told about my sister's death and that I wasn't going to her funeral, nor would I be going anywhere except to a Christian dorm with a bunch of ladies who I didn't know and didn't want to know. I was so hurt and angry, and, to make matters worse, the girls in the dorm must have been told about me coming and started apologizing for my sister's death, telling me how sorry they were about her dying. One girl in particular was eating as she was saying how sorry she was for my sister dying, but as she was saying that, she was spitting food from her mouth onto me. I wanted to hit her, beat her up, but as I stood there, wanting to die, the dorm mom, who was another inmate, told everyone to leave me alone. She told them to let me be with God and not to bother me. I felt so alone. What did she mean "be with God"; how do you do that?

I looked up the stairs to the second floor. There was one place at the top I spotted and thought maybe I could simply go there and have a reprieve from flying food particles. As I walked up the stairs, so much pain came flooding into my body. It was like every bit of pain from my past to this point surfaced; it hurt so badly. I was like a cartoon of a person who had been shot with a cannonball that went right through them and left a huge hole. I looked to see if the second floor was high enough to jump off and kill myself, but it looked like I would simply break something and not die.

As I sat down, all the girls on the top floor moved down the stairs and were talking and sitting at the table with the dorm mom. I looked at where I was and what had happened. I don't know if you have ever hurt this badly emotionally, but I am telling you that not one place in my body wasn't filled with anguish. I was hurting before, but this was such a great pain that it was excruciating. I could hardly speak. I remembered the words I had said to God, "I didn't really get saved because of You. I really got saved to be with Jackie, but if You are real like You say You are, then I need You to either kill me or touch me, because I hurt so bad I can't take it."

At that very moment when I said that, it was like a wind came from somewhere. The Bible states in John 3:8, "The wind blows wherever it pleases. You hear its sound, but you don't know where the wind comes from or where it's going. That's the way it is with everyone born of the Spirit."

Also, the Holy Spirit on the day of Pentecost came as a mighty rushing wind. I felt the wind of the Holy Spirit." He engulfed me with His presence. The experience made me gasp, and I sat up straight because of this wonderful presence that was filling my very being. I was looking around to see where this wind and presence had come from. I say wind because it's the best way I can describe what had happened to me. I felt like something was blowing on me and through me, but I felt for certain that something wonderful had just touched me. In fact, that wonderful presence was coming up through my body and resounded throughout my whole being. All the sorrow and all the pain turned into a joy and peace that is simply indescribable. It was like nothing that I had ever experienced before. With all the drugs that I have done, all the money I spent to get high, nothing was like what I experienced. It was God; I felt Him and His Holy Spirit.

If God had said I should go away from Him, it would have been right. After all, I was in jail—a prisoner, a criminal. That is what I deserved. That would have been just in my eyes, but God didn't do that. Instead, He came to me and He didn't say go away. He said to come and to draw near. He drew so near that He engulfed me with Himself. He didn't send me away. He was glad to see me and touch me in all my mess. God Himself sent His Son to justify me, to judge me as not guilty. I didn't deserve what He was giving me, but I thank God for his Son Jesus and that through Him we are saved and so loved.

I got so excited that all my anguish left me. I said with such excitement and great joy, "You really are alive!"

The more I proclaimed Him being alive the more alive He became to me. The joy that filled my heart made me laugh and smile, and I felt His presence. This one touch from God changed me forever. The Bible states that the Kingdom of God is peace, joy, and righteousness. I was looking peace, joy, and righteousness directly in the face. It was Jesus. He is all those things.

He didn't turn me away. Now that everything I had believed was false was staring me directly in the face, there was no way to deny that Jesus was real, because I had just met Him face-to-face. Now I knew, the Bible was true, He is real, and since He is real that means everything that He says is true. When He said that He had forgiven me of all my sins, He did. When He said that I was a new creation, I was changed inside out to be like Him, and that means it is true. But the greatest of all was when I realized I would get to be with Him and see my sister again, and, yes, all my sins, all the terrible things, were forgiven.

The more I thought about those things and said those things, the more joy filled my heart and all the pain was gone. I lit up like a light bulb, or even like a lighthouse. I could feel Him and could tell that a great Light had come. The power of God was in me, and after that, for months, I could feel Him in me.

The thing I noticed about God right away was that He is love. He cared. He didn't look down on me; He was happy and excited to come to me. He ran to me. In the story of the prodigal son, when he returned to his father, the Bible states that when the father saw him from afar, he picked up his tunic or robe so he could really run to reach his son. He ran as fast as he could to go embrace his son. His son who was lost was now found. Consider this: the Bible states that his son was among pigs, eating with pigs, so he smelled like a pig, had dirt and pig dung all over him. The Bible says that the father embraced and kissed his son, because he had his son back. The father kissed his son even with pig dung on his face, and the father didn't care.

Jesus was the same with me. I didn't look good or smell too good, but He didn't care. He ran to me that day and embraced me and kissed me. God wasn't only full of love but He was also full of joy that He shared with me. He filled me with joy that was overwhelming joy, unspeakable joy. There was so much joy—it made me strong and empowered me. No wonder the Bible states that the joy of the Lord is our strength, because I felt strong. I was experiencing the Kingdom of Light now, instead of what I had been so used to all those years, the kingdom of darkness. Now I had love, joy, peace, and righteousness, instead of despair, death, and depression. I knew that no matter what I faced ahead, I would never go back to where I had come from. I knew I was set free. I knew heaven had touched me, and I had just met the Holy Spirit of God.

In II Corinthians 5:17 the Bible states, "Therefore if any person is [ingrafted] in Christ (the Messiah) he is a new creation (a new creature altogether); the old [previous moral and spiritual condition] has passed away. Behold, the fresh and new has come!"

This is one of my favorite verses in the Bible because I became this new creation because of the Creator Himself. Just like the beginning of time, when the Holy Spirit hovered over nothing then created the worlds and the heavens, He hovered over nothing and turned a nothing into a child of God. In reality, I was in prison, but in the Spirit I was in His Kingdom. I was new, I was free, and the prison doors had been opened, even though in reality, they were still locked.

I never mourned my sister after that day, and I was never the same. I was so excited that He is alive and He, Jesus, is really the Son of God. After finding out the truth, nothing else mattered. I told Him from that day forward that I would serve Him all the days of my life, and after seventeen years with Him, I have never left Him or gone back to the way I used to be.

To be honest, I would rather die than to ever go back to life without Jesus. Without Him, life isn't life at all. So many people think they live life. I don't care who you are. You can have all the power in the world, all the money to buy anything you want. You might be famous, but none of that matters if you don't have Jesus. There was no other name I cried out to, not anyone or anything, only Jesus, and He answered me. No one can tell me He isn't real, I know firsthand He is! All those years and money spent trying to get help were wasted time. One touch from the Lord changed everything. If He can change me, He can change anyone. It is amazing and wonderful what has happened to me, and it can happen to you also.

The next time I went to church in jail, after being touched by God, I saw my partner in crime, who was no longer my partner in crime, but my sister in Christ. She had not seen me since my experience with the living God, so when I walked into the chapel she freaked out, and others that had seen me in the dorm where they moved from were completely amazed when I walked in. They exclaimed, "You got touched by God!" Everything began to change from that day. That day of pain turned into great joy. For the first time in my life, I felt freedom. Even though I was behind bars, I felt more freedom than I had ever felt in my life beyond jail. I was in jail, but free. I wasn't in the prison of shame and guilt or the prison of addiction anymore, because whomever the Son sets free is free indeed (John 8:36).

Chapter 8

New Creation

Therefore if any person is in Christ he is a new creation
(a new creature altogether); the old previous moral and
spiritual condition has passed away, behold the fresh
and new has come!

(II Corinthians 5:17)

After being touched by God, I was different. I would look at myself
in the fake mirrors they have in jail and ask myself, "Who are you?"
There was such a drastic change in me that it freaked me out, especially
when it came to craving drugs, or even having any thoughts of drugs.
All the addiction was gone. The addiction to drinking, smoking, and
drugs was gone. I would even try purposely to think about drugs, and
the thoughts just weren't there. This newfound freedom was nothing I
had ever experienced in my life. All those years I did drugs, I had spent
all that money for something fake and unreal. Now I had the real high,
the real happiness, and the feeling of fitting in that I searched for so
desperately all those years. I found my home in Him.

I don't want to give the impression that all of a sudden I was just
perfect and everything in my life had changed. Honestly, in the spirit,

all things were made new, but I had to find that out. I was far from being perfect. In fact, the deliverance that I experienced was an awesome gift. It was free, and Jesus died on the cross for me to have that. I was thirty-six when I got saved, and of those thirty-six years, half of those years were spent using drugs and drinking. I was a mess. There were a lot of lies implanted in me that the truth of God's Word had to begin to expel. That is the true process of being a Christian.

Recently I noticed that all my drawers in my desk and bedroom were a mess, so I took the time to clean them up, throw away what was not needed and re-organized all my things. It's amazing how easy life is now. I can find what I need and there is less confusion.

That is a perfect example of what God does within us. He takes all the mess and unwanted things that will get in the way of what is supposed to be there. These things can cause confusion and makes it hard for us to find Him. When you find your way, you can help others.

If you don't allow the Holy Spirit to do the cleaning and organizing in you, then it's like having a messy closet. Along comes a friend who stops by and wants to borrow a sweater. You send her to your closet, she opens the closet door, but then closes it immediately because all your things begin falling on top of her. Everything comes out but the sweater that she wanted.

The Holy Spirit wants to clean and organize your closet. So, whatever we have to help others is what comes out because it is organized and easy to find. God keeps what you need and discards what you don't. I call it "garbage in, garbage out." The devil puts lies in, and He, the Spirit of Truth, removes the lies and replaces them with the Truth. It is similar to replacing the memory on a computer's hard drive. When you do that, the information being entered into the computer is entirely new, not the same. This is another perfect example of how the Word of God works in our lives.

Earlier in my story, I said the drugs had moved in and I moved out. Well now, with the new creation, the darkness moved out and Jesus moved in. The drugs moved out and the light moved in. How awesome that is!

Now the real work of the Holy Spirit would continue day-by-day, hour-by-hour, and sometimes, moment-by-moment. The drugs were just a symptom of the real issues. Though I had been delivered of my addictions, I was still a mess. The Bible is like a mirror, so every time you look into it, you see areas that need to be changed. Is this meant to hurt us? Heavens no! It is to improve us from glory to glory and faith to faith. That's the restoration process.

The experience I had in the spirit translated me out of darkness into His very light. That very moment when I received Jesus as my Lord and Savior, I was changed and taken from a pit to a palace. Just like the prodigal son, I went from a pigpen to a palace. Jesus took me from the pit that I was in and placed me right beside Him in the heavenly places. The problem is that I still saw myself in the pit. I was still in jail, my sister had just died, and I was looking at forty years in prison. What was so wonderful was that I wasn't alone anymore. This time, even though I thought I was in a pit, I had steps that were lit now so I could see my way out of this pit. God was showing me the way up and out through His Word, and He was walking with me, holding my hand as I went up the stairway.

Here is a great example of what happened to me. If you take a drink from a bottle of spring or purified water, that water is usually bottled in a recycled container. You are drinking from a container that has been transformed into something entirely different. In fact, if you knew what the bottle had been before, you might not drink the water in that bottle. Second Corinthians 3:18 states, "All of us, as with unveiled face, (because we) continued to behold (in the Word of God) as in a mirror the glory of the Lord are constantly being transfigured into His very own image in ever increasing splendor and from one degree of glory to another, (for this comes) from the Lord (who is) the Spirit." We are changed or transformed into the image of the Son of God.

I became like that recycled bottle. What I was, I wasn't anymore. What I used to like, I didn't like anymore. Before, I didn't care about the Bible. Now, I couldn't stay away from it. I would actually fall asleep with it some nights. What a contrast! Before, I would stay awake doing drugs, now I am staying awake spending time with my newfound Friend and reading His Word. The more I stayed in His Word, the more I was being transformed—being changed or recycled. I was like a caterpillar that was changed into a butterfly. When you look up the word "changed" or "transformed" in Greek, it means I am being metamorphosed into the image of God.

But, everything was not wonderful in my life. I still had a long road ahead of me. A lot of times people think that when you become a Christian, all your problems are over and you just walk around in this unrealistic, euphoric state praising God all day. That is not the case. In fact, you might even have more problems because now you have really made the devil mad because you have switched sides. You no longer belong to him. Now, you belong to Jesus.

If you think the enemy of your soul is just going to lie down and let you have everything that the Lord provides without a fight, you are mistaken. I found that out the hard way. In fact, the fight is underway, but what is so great is that you are not fighting alone. When you learn more and more about the Bible, you find that our God has given us every possible weapon to win our battles.

Why am I sharing my story? Well, it's not just *my* story, as it belongs to the Lord. I must tell you that Jesus Christ is still in the miracle-working business. He isn't dead. He is still alive and His Word is still alive, and he is able to do the impossible. If I had not received a miracle and had an encounter with Jesus Christ, I would not be alive today. Many people I know who went back to the drugs and that kind of life are dead or are spending the rest of their lives behind bars. People have to know the saying, "Once an addict always an addict," is not true. I am proof of that. I found out later, after being released from prison, that only six percent of people who were as addicted to drugs as I was actually make it. The rest die or are locked away forever.

It doesn't have to be like that. It wasn't AA or NA or anything else that set me free. It was Jesus Christ. Simply believe in Him and He will change the impossible into possible. I was impossible! I have found in my life that Jesus is always more willing to work than we are willing to give Him an opportunity to work.

Some people say that I got free because I was incarcerated. No, it took the incarceration to make me quiet enough to hear God. It wasn't jail that set me free; it was Jesus, my newfound Friend. The benefit of incarceration was that now I had time to learn more about this new freedom. When the chaplains of the jail and the church lady, Jan, moved me into the Christian dorm, I became more involved than ever with the Word of God. In fact, I knew something was really going on with me, because I didn't want to do anything but read my Bible. I did one Bible study after another. Night and day, I would spend time in the Word of God. I just wanted to know more and more about this Word of God.

In some jails they give you a box to hold your things. You push it under your bunk. I would take and sit on my box and use my bunk as a desk. In my room, there was this little window maybe about three inches wide and about a foot or two long. When I sat on my box on the floor, I could see clouds and the sky. Sometimes I would see a bird fly by. I would look up to heaven and just talk to the Lord. I would cry and thank Him for what He had done for me. I don't know how to explain the relief that I felt. I didn't know what was ahead of me, but I just knew it was going to be OK.

True repentance is a true turning from all you are to all Jesus is. True repentance will make you do things differently. As the Bible says, "Repent, for the kingdom of God is at hand" (Matthew 3:2).

Repenting means more than being sorry for your sins or mistakes, or being sorry you got caught. When I got arrested, I had no interest in changing. I was simply sorry I got caught. Repentance is that, no matter what, I turned from the way I was doing things to doing things a whole new way—God's way. I found out that the Word of God was my new road map for life; my "owner's manual" for this new being I had become.

For the next four months or so, I spent all my days and nights in classes learning about the Word of God, going to church, and doing Bible studies. I completed so many Bible studies that the chaplain of the jail purchased a Bible with her own money to reward me for completing a whole series. That was my first personal Bible, and I was so proud of it. I still remember the scripture she inscribed in the front of that Bible, one that I could hold onto throughout the ordeal I was about to face. She wrote: "Psalm 27:1 'The Lord is my Light and Salvation—whom shall I fear or dread? The Lord is the Refuge and Stronghold of my life—of whom shall I be afraid?'"

Little did I know that this verse was preparing me for what was about to come my way, the temptations that I would face, the sentencing that was near, and the evil that waited for me in the other county where I would be sent.

Chapter 9

The Priceless Pearl

When he found one priceless pearl, he went and sold everything he had and bought it.

(Matthew 13:46, HCSB)

Looking back, I know God was involved in the arrest process when I was arrested in Seminole County instead of Polk County, where I came from. Honestly, if I had been arrested in Polk County instead of Seminole, I wouldn't be here to write this book. During all my arrests in Polk County, there was not a church like in Seminole County. The church they did have was hard to get to because it was held in a drunk tank and only a few people could fit in the classroom at one time. However I do remember church ladies who would go from cell to cell and see if anyone wanted to have a prayer session.

The old Polk County Jail was awful, and I was about to go there again. I know jail is supposed to be an awful experience so that maybe you won't come back, but I was coming from the security of a Christian dorm and a Christian program, leaving a place that was all about the Word of God, and going to a place that was all about my past and old ways.

I think of my experience with the Lord like a great awakening. I remember seeing this movie called *Awakenings*, starring Robin Williams and Robert DeNiro. In this movie, Robin Williams played a doctor and Robert DeNiro played a patient who contracted a disease that put him in a catatonic state. He was in a coma for many years. After all those years, the doctor discovered a cure and healed his patient. After those many years, the patient had to experience life all over again, as if he had never existed. When he woke up from the coma, he had to learn everything again, even riding a bus and going to the grocery store. Everything to him was a brand new experience. This is how it was for me. For eighteen years I had lived in a catatonic type state. I had been in a "coma" from drugs and all the other terrible things I had done. When I met Jesus, everything was new and I had to learn how to handle this new life I had been given. I had to learn to walk, talk, hear, and touch. Everything had changed, and I had to learn everything from scratch.

I remember the horrid smell of the Polk County jail. The cells were small with showers and bathrooms wide open for all to see. The bars were old steel bars, so you could reach through to hand someone something, but you could also see anyone showering or going to the bathroom. I had experienced this place six times, and now I was coming back to it again. But this time, I was different. I had no idea how difficult it was going to be this time around. No church, no Christian fellowship, and, worst of all, all the people who I had used drugs with were there. The guards also knew me from before because I had been processed in while they were there.

I was scared. I didn't know if I could handle going back to where I had come from. I had survived my sister's death about four or five months before, and now I was going from a type of heaven back to the pit. I didn't want to go, but my life wasn't my own. I was state *and* federal property, so I did what they said and went where they sent me.

I thank God to this day that He heard my mom's prayers to save her little girl. I also know that God didn't cause me to get arrested. It was my choices that got me arrested. He intervened in such a manner that He had that police officer be at that very spot, at that very time, and in the that particular county so that He could get me and keep me forever.

I was sentenced in Seminole County, and I was sad that the sentence was so light. This was because of the other charges I had against me elsewhere. They figured that letting another county pay for me would be better for them. My time of being in the surroundings of the Lord and peace were coming to an end.

I said good-bye to Chaplain Westmoreland. To this day, I have never forgotten her. After all, she was the one who introduced me to Jesus, my new Friend. At one point, I wanted to be just like her. I thought it was cool that she preached and played the guitar. Chaplain Westmoreland helped me memorize so many scriptures through her way of turning the Word of God into songs. I especially remember Galatians 2:20: "I am crucified with Christ nevertheless I live, it's not I but Christ who liveth in me, and the life of flesh I use to live, I live by the faith of the Son of God who loves me and gave Himself for me." This scripture was set to this catchy tune, and I still sing it to this day, because of her.

I was on my way now. The handcuffs and shackles were placed on me and the van arrived to get me to take me back to Polk County. To ride in the back of a jail van is quite an experience. On either side inside the van are built-in cages that can fit three to four people on each side. Toward the front of the van is a section for men, who are only separated by wire. The space has enough room for your knees. I felt bad for larger people and taller people, because you were like sardines in that van. Your hands are handcuffed and then connected to the shackles around your feet, so moving around is difficult. Long distances are very uncomfortable, and many parts of your body fall asleep. I had about a two-hour drive with no stops, so I was praying a lot.

I can't tell you the thoughts I was having as we traveled down the highway. I kept repeating the scriptures that had been given to me, especially this one: "The Lord is my Light and Salvation, of whom shall I be afraid" (Psalms 27:1). I was praying for the Lord to keep me strong and for me to be guided by Him to reach others, but, honestly, I was scared and wanted Him to help me. I couldn't do this alone and I knew that.

When we arrived at Polk County Jail, I stepped out of the van and was taken into the booking area. After many hours in a holding cell, I was finger-printed and officially charged with sixteen charges of various crimes, mainly theft. Each time the charges were read to me, I had to remind myself that I was a new person and the Lord had forgiven me. The full meaning of knowing I was forgiven of all my sins had not gotten deep into my heart, even though I had heard it. It has taken a lot of years for the understanding of God's forgiveness to get down deep inside me. Some days, I don't feel forgiven or saved, but Christianity and the work of the cross are not about our feelings. It's all about what Jesus accomplished when He went to the cross. I had done a lot of wrong, and to know that I was forgiven was going to take more than hearing it a few times.

I was led upstairs to the cells. I was totally undone when they put me in the dorm I would be in until I was sentenced. I couldn't believe how I felt. I was like a fish out of water. I was so different by then that I didn't fit into that environment anymore. Less than a year before, I had been a lot like what I was seeing of the girls in the cellblock, but now I was like an outsider looking in on such evil that it overwhelmed me. I climbed up on the top bunk and looked around at all the cussing, fighting, and screaming. This was what I used to be like. It was apparent to me that I didn't like this anymore, but I didn't have much of a choice. How would I adjust to this? I had this priceless pearl inside me now, this precious Holy Spirit, who I was just getting to know, but I didn't want to harm Him. It was if I was trying to protect Him, even though I was the one who needed protecting. I didn't know what to do, so I sat in the corner on the top bunk and drew myself up like a ball and prayed, "Oh God, help me!"

I was so scared of this new environment that I couldn't even read my Bible. It was as if I had never committed a crime before.

Separation is not a bad word, nor was it something bad for me to be separated from the environment I was in at Polk County. But, what good is it to take a little plant that has just started growing out of the dirt and place it in the dark again? It most surely will die. The new seedling needs plenty of light, warmth, security, and water for it to live. I was like that little plant.

The moment I asked Jesus to come into my heart and forgive me of my sins, His supernatural powers began to work on me to change me into His image. All those months I was in Seminole County, I was hanging around God and His Word. What you hang around is what you become.

After I gave my life to the Lord, for four or five months, I was hanging around God, and He had rubbed off on me. He is the Priceless Pearl, and I was and am still willing to sell anything and everything to get that Priceless Pearl.

If I was willing to walk through a tropical storm to get dope, then how much more am I going to do to go after God? I knew that if I ever went back to the way I had been, then I would die. Yet, it wasn't fear that had me stay with Jesus. I loved Him, and not only did I love Him but I also liked Him.

I just knew He had touched me and I wasn't the same. I didn't want those girls who were like I used to be to rub off on me. I was still new, only five months old—only five months out of my coma. I didn't want anything to ruin it.

Now, when the church ladies came from cell to cell to ask if anyone wanted prayer, I would jump off my bunk and run to them. I was desperate for Christian fellowship, and I couldn't wait to get to church. I needed that spiritual food more than I did real food. It wasn't long before I just couldn't take the cell I was in any longer. I prayed and asked the Lord to help me to be freed so I could be with Him. So even though I knew it was going to be hard, I decided to ask God if He would let me go to isolation. Isolation is for people who fear for their safety, but I was trying to protect my spiritual well-being. It was worth it for me to protect and seek after that Priceless Pearl.

When I got the nerve, I went to the cell and waited eagerly for the officer to come by. Yes, here she came, and I felt she was favorable toward me. I asked the officer on duty if she would please move me to another cell. She looked at me seriously and asked me if I was suicidal, and I responded politely with "No, Ma'am."

Then she said, "Do you fear for your safety?" and I said, "No, Ma'am, but I do fear for my spiritual well-being."

As she walked away I didn't get an answer, but I thought to myself, *Oh well, I tried.* That night they came and told me to pack up. I was moving. They moved me to isolation, all by myself in a cell with no one to talk to—just my Bible, my Priceless Pearl, and me. It would be months before I would be back in general population, but those months with the Lord were heavenly.

I called my cell "my apartment." I would take toothpaste, which I used as glue, and put scriptures all over my apartment walls. When I wasn't fasting and praying, I was singing and worshiping the Lord. I didn't know a lot of songs, but I would sing anyway. I don't have enough time here to tell you about all the miracles the Lord did for me during those months that I was alone with Him. It was my first Christmas being saved and one of my best Christmases ever because now I understood that Christmas is about the Lord, who I had just recently met. I just loved singing Happy Birthday to Him. I wasn't even sad to be alone because I was so happy to be different from the way I had been.

I remember one miracle that I greatly appreciated. When you are in jail and someone leaves to go home, you can trade your mattress or whatever you need for a better one. I had a terrible mattress. My hips hurt so badly. The mattress was super thin and it lay on a metal bed. After the months of sleeping on this metal bed, my body was really starting to hurt.

So, I remembered the Bible states that I can ask for whatever I need and the Lord will supply it for me. I asked the Lord for a new mattress. The mattress I wanted was a new, thick, green mattress that was so much softer than what I had. I asked God for a new, thick, green mattress.

One day, I went to the rec area to get some fresh air. While I was gone, the guard on duty put a new mattress in my cell. When they brought me back to the cell, I flipped out. I went and jumped on the mattress, but, unfortunately, it was like my old one. It was new and green but not fluffy. I could tell the Lord was trying to teach me to ask specifically in my prayers, so I asked again.

When the officer came back, I asked her if she had done that for me and she said yes. I thanked her so much and she asked me how it was. I told her the truth, that it was still flat and hard. She looked around to see if anyone else was around, then she opened my cell door and told me to hurry around the corner with her. As I went around the corner, there, before my eyes, were stacks of fluffy, green mattresses. The area was overflowing with mattresses. The officer told me to take my pick but to hurry. I was so happy! I asked God to help me pick the right one. The rest of my stay, which was months, was on a comfortable new, green, fluffy mattress.

God blessed me with new friends from the outside world. Some Christian ladies would come and bring me reading material. Miss Lois became a dear friend who always brought me reading material about faith, healing, the baptism of the Holy Spirit, and identity in Christ. She was a kind mentor. Miss Lois introduced me to great men and women of God, like Brother Hagin and Kenneth and Gloria Copeland, and brought me some books by Joyce Meyer.

God also brought me another dear friend, Aleta. I remember the first time I saw her preaching with Miss Lois in the drunk tank at the Polk County Jail. Aleta was alight with God and she was so beautiful. I was so drawn to her. I wasn't attracted to her because she was pretty. It was simply the femininity and the presence of God in her. I wanted to be just like her. I wondered, *Can I be pretty like that, will I look like this when I grow up in the Lord?*

As I sat on the floor listening to her, I told the Lord that I wanted to be just like her. I wanted to be pretty and feminine and love Him as she did. I also wanted to be on fire for God the way she was. I can say that He has answered my prayer after all these years. Not to brag, but the Lord has done a great job with me. I love being a woman of God. I love the work of the Lord in my life.

As you know, my sister died three days after I got saved. It had been almost eight months since her departure to heaven when my mom became ill. It was a combination of the eighteen years of abuse and pain I put her through and losing Jackie. My mom loved us, and Jackie was very special to her. They spoke daily even though my sister lived in Indiana. Jackie was sick growing up, so that brought them closer together. Also, when I was born, my mom received a blood transfusion. She contracted hepatitis from the transfusion but didn't know about it until much later when the damage had already been done. My mom's liver became damaged so much so that she developed cirrhosis of the liver. I remember my mom getting really mad if a doctor asked her if she drank liquor. My mom had a brother who was an alcoholic *and* a daughter with drug and alcohol problems. The last thing she wanted was alcohol! She responded nicely but firmly telling the doctor no over and over again. For years my mom was fine, but after my sentencing and my sister's death, it was just too much for her.

I was in my isolation cell, and I had asked numerous times to use the phone to call my mom. I just had a feeling that something wasn't right. I repeatedly called out again and again, trying to reach someone, but to no avail. After many attempts, I started to pray. It wasn't long before my mentor Miss Lois came to my cell. I knew something was wrong. She took my hand and told me that my mom was in intensive care with liver failure and she was hemorrhaging to the point of near death. She also told me that she had a ten percent chance of making it, and that was a just an estimation. Miss Lois left and told me she would be back after she made her rounds at the jail to check on me.

My heart left my body. I was overwhelmed with that hopeless feeling again and with grief. I grabbed my Bible, went to the corner of my cell, slid down the wall, and began to cry.

As I cried, I heard in my heart from the Holy Spirit, "Get up."

I said, "What?"

He said, "Get up."

So, I wiped my tears and crawled on my knees with the Bible in my hands. When I reached my bunk, I opened my Bible, and there was my mom's thread. There were times when my mom would come and get my undergarments and t-shirts. One time when my mom had brought back my washing with freshly cleaned garments, I saw one of her threads on the clothes. I had taken that thread and put it in my Bible. It was the closest thing I had to my mom, and it was a comfort to me. I didn't know it, but I had put that thread in the chapter where the Lord heals the lady with the issue of blood.

When I opened my Bible and I saw my mom's thread I began to read the story, found in Mark 5:25-34, of a women who had suffered at the hands of many physicians. Well, that was my mom. She had gone to many doctors, but none could help her. Then, I kept reading that she was bleeding to death. Well, that was my mom too. She was hemorrhaging and no one could stop it. The lady in the story said, "If only I could touch the hem of His garment, then I would be whole." I was overwhelmed. Jesus told the women after she had reached out and touched Him that her faith had made her whole. I could feel faith rising up in me. I told the Lord, "OK, Lord, my mom can't reach out and touch You, but I can for her." As I reached out, pretending to touch the hem of His garment, I could feel His hand on my shoulder. I could feel a hand touch me, and, at that moment, I knew He had healed my mom. I started rejoicing and singing praises to my God, my

Lord. I didn't see it but I knew that He heard my prayer because I felt Him touch my shoulder. I stood up and started dancing around my cell just shouting and singing.

When Miss Lois came back, she was expecting to minister to me for depression, but instead I was happy and laughing, and I told her my mom was healed. That night I got through to my family. My mom had been moved from the intensive care unit to a regular room. Two weeks later she was playing golf with my dad again. Praise God! That Priceless Pearl, Jesus, is worth giving up everything for. He is still the same as He was before. He still works miracles, and I am one of His miracles. There is nothing impossible for Him to change or do, and I am proof of that. He cannot fail. We might fail Him, but He can't fail us. His Word is true, and I am proof of that.

Chapter 10

The Sentence

I have gone through a lot of healing while writing this book and have worried about what people might think of me. I thank God for the Holy Spirit who helps us to overcome all our weaknesses. I read somewhere that your past is simply a story and that once you realize this, it has no power over you. My past has no power over me, and that is freedom. In everything, I thank God. When I allow Him to have it all, good, bad, ugly, past, present, and future, nothing is wasted. He will use it for His glory. As long as I glorify my God and let people know how amazing He is by offering encouragement and hope instead of despair, then I have succeeded in what God has led me to do.

I heard a wise woman of God say, "Let your mess become God's message." So, here is my mess that God is using for His message. And what is His message? With God, all things are possible. Boy, what a mess I made in life. As you know, I was arrested in April 1997. In early 1998, I was still in the Polk County jail. I hadn't touched the grass, seen the moon and the stars, or hugged my mom for almost a year. I would smell my mom's scent on my undergarments that she so graciously washed for me. "My apartment" was starting to close in on me. It was time for me to push my way out of my cocoon of safety and face the giant ahead of me.

The Bible proclaims that everything becomes new when you give your life to Jesus. I thought that everything was going to be easy and life would just turn into a wonderful euphoric state, but that is not how it works. When you become a Christian, it doesn't mean you are not going to face challenges in your life. Jesus Himself even said in John 16:33 in *The Message* Bible, "In this godless world you will continue to experience difficulties. But take heart! I've conquered the world."

What most of us don't understand is that there are consequences for our sins, even though we are forgiven. If I had sex outside of marriage and got pregnant, then gave my life to the Lord and repented of the sin, I am forgiven, but I am still pregnant.

When you throw a stone into a still, clear pond, it has a ripple effect. The ripples move across the pond. When we sin, those ripples go out and affect everything in their path. Yet, on the other side of it, when we receive Jesus and we let Him change and restore us, those ripples become ripples of life and restoration instead of death and destruction. Whatever our sins are, however difficult the path is, there is provision and restoration through Jesus. He won't leave you or forsake you. He will walk with you every step of your journey.

So, I raised my hand to receive Jesus. At that moment, He forgave me for all my sins past and present. I was new on the inside, but I had to pay for my crimes, and that is good. As you will see, our God is merciful. His mercies are new every day. Thank God, because I needed mercy.

I had sixteen charges in Polk county. With six prior arrests, things didn't look promising for me. In the state of Florida, whether you are to be sentenced to prison or not, it is based on a point system. Therefore, when you reach a certain number of points, you are going to jail no matter what. I had so many points that I exceeded the number needed to be incarcerated. The state kept trying to sentence me to prison time with a lot of probation. But, I still had federal charges to face and, most likely, federal prison time as well. I prayed and I felt that I was simply to do prison time and not be released with probation hanging over my head. So, I declined every offer with probation connected to it. With great respect to the court, I said no, and then asked the judge to please simply give me prison time only.

With that, I learned a lot about patience. God showed me to live each day as one day and not look at tomorrow because I had a lot of tomorrows locked behind bars. It was a relief to just say, "OK, God, I will not count my days anymore; I will just stay in today." And, with His help, I did just that.

After months of serving my time, an offer came my way. I couldn't believe what God did. The Lord was so kind to me when it came to my state charges. I had sixteen charges. Each charge by itself could be a minimum of a year each, or a maximum of five years each. Thanks to God, the judge combined all my charges into *one* charge. As a result, I was sentenced to two years state prison with "gaintime" for the time I had spent in jail. (According to the Florida Department of Corrections, gaintime is an inmate's opportunity to earn a sentence reduction.) I would do a year and a half in a state facility. When the sentencing was over, I was relieved. Now, I had one more giant to face: the federal charges. I had no idea what I was actually facing or just how tough things would become for me.

God knew what was ahead of me, and I would not exchange what I learned in the years I spent in prison for any amount of money. Prison is not rehabilitation. It's created to punish and, most likely, keep a person in the system. I was determined that, no matter what, I was not going to leave this place the same way I came in. In fact, I asked the Lord to not let me out again if I was going to go back to the way I used to be. I would rather die than to ever go back to that living hell I had made for myself.

Incarceration was tough, but I learned about the faithfulness of God and how great He really is. Jesus was with me every step of the way. I wanted to be changed body, mind, and spirit. I always tell people I didn't go to prison; I went to Bible school with a great security system that kept all the bad people out. I met some of the nicest people behind bars. Sure, there were some mean ones, but, for the most part, they were hurt. Hurting people hurt other people. You wouldn't believe the talent and abilities that these men and women behind bars have. I truly believe that when a prisoner is saved, filled with the Holy Spirit, and on fire for God, you've got yourself a weapon of mass destruction against the kingdom of darkness. We know what the enemy is like. We have worked for him for a long time. So, what better person to enlist in the army of God than traitors from the other side? We know Satan's tactics and aren't afraid to be in God's Special Forces unit and get our hands dirty. We are willing to go to the trenches where a lot of church-goers don't want to go.

There is a lot to say about the word "determination." What a great word! When you become a Christian, no matter what you face, you must be determined to not quit. There were so many times in the seventeen years I have been with the Lord that I wanted to quit. Not quit God, but quit *life*. I don't mean suicide; I have asked the Lord, "Can you just take me home now?" But, I am still here, and I will see this race through to the finish no matter what.

I looked up the word "determination." All the meanings lead to one thing: determination is simply not giving up. Determination is not letting go. It's falling on your face and getting back up again. This word is powerful, and there is not one single person in the Bible who didn't have determination. Jesus was determined to reach Calvary while carrying that cruel cross for us. Paul was determined to preach the gospel of Jesus Christ even after being shipwrecked—not once but many times, after being in the ocean night and day before being rescued. Moses was determined to lead God's people to the Promised Land.

But, what about us? We must be determined not to give up. When things get tough and you just want to let everything go and give up, that is the time to be determined. You are almost there! Determination is being willing to keep going, to keep pushing and pressing on, and one day it will be worth it. I like the movie *Finding Nemo*. It's one of my favorite movies. There is one scene when Dory starts singing, "Just keep swimming, just keep swimming!" Dory sang that over and over again. So, let us be determined and just keep swimming!

After the sentencing, I was led back to my cell and I felt I needed to praise and thank God, but something was missing. There was something I knew that God wanted to do for me. Our God equips us with His power to overcome. He won't ask us to give up something without replacing it with double or more. He takes things out of us to fill us up with Him. A full glass can't contain anything more because it is full. But, when you pour out the contents of that glass, then you can fill it again. That is how God is with us. That's the true work of the Holy Spirit and the life of a true Christian, when you allow Him to empty you so He can fill you up with Him. He, the Holy Spirit, wants to consume your total being, and, if you allow Him to, He will make you new on the inside.

I could feel that the Lord wanted to do something with me that day. While in isolation, there was a girl who was saved in the cell beside me. We would talk sometimes even though we couldn't see each other. I would hear her pray in a funny language; I was hungry to know what it was. One day I asked her what kind of language it was. She told me she was speaking in tongues and that she was praying in her own heavenly language. I wanted to know more. So, the church lady who was mentoring me brought some books on the baptism of the Holy Spirit. The more I read the more I wanted to speak in tongues. I read that when you are baptized with the Holy Spirit, this language is the one God uses to speak through you. The Book of Acts describes what happened to all the disciples on Pentecost. All the disciples of Jesus received the baptism of the Holy Spirit. John the Baptist proclaimed in Matthew 3:11 that he baptized with water, but Jesus would baptize with the Holy Spirit and with fire. This was the best thing I have ever heard. I wanted the Holy Spirit, and I had the Holy Spirit when I got saved. He, the Spirit of Christ, came and started to reside in me. He is what brought the instant change in me. In fact, it was the precious Holy Spirit who touched me that day at the top of those stairs that changed me forever.

I wanted Him. I was so hungry; I asked for the Holy Spirit so many times, but no speaking in tongues. I was getting discouraged. I thought maybe the Lord just didn't want to give Him to me. *The devil is such a liar*, I thought. Maybe I just did too much wrong to receive that. But, on that day, I said "no, that can't be it." The girl in the other cell could speak in tongues and she had committed a crime. On that day, I was reading a book about the Holy Spirit, and it said that if I wasn't speaking in tongues, then I didn't have the Holy Spirit. I was as mad as fire.

I threw that book down and got on my knees by my bunk, and I told the Lord with great zeal, "I know I have the Holy Spirit because I am saved!" What is up, Lord? I want to speak with tongues. I want you to baptize me in the Holy Spirit. I want the Holy Spirit!" I exclaimed.

All of the sudden I heard the Lord very gently tell me to be quiet. Then, He said, "Open your mouth," and when I did, all of a sudden the most wonderful thing started to happen to me.

I started praying in an unknown tongue I didn't understand. In fact, it sounded like gibberish, it made no sense. It almost sounded like Chinese—it's beautiful. It was glorious. It seemed I only said one syllable for the longest time, and I was afraid to move. My knees were hurting from being on the cement floor so long, but I didn't know anything. I was afraid if I moved He would stop, but that wasn't the case at all. I prayed so much; it felt so good. I was laughing, crying, and praying all at the same time. The girl next door to me started praising God and thanking the Lord that I had received the baptism of the Holy Spirit. It wasn't long before my one syllable changed. Then, beautiful Hebrew sound started coming out of me. Oh, it was a great experience. And, it didn't just happen once! I could pray at will. I would just let the Lord have His way. I prayed and prayed in the Holy Spirit, and I kept reading about how the devil didn't know what I was saying. I didn't know either, but I was tickled pink to know that stupid jerk had no idea what was going on. I was happy about that; anything to pay him back for all he has done to me.

There are some wonderful miracles that the Lord has allowed me to experience with Him. In fact, my whole life is a miracle. The greatest miracle of all is salvation, but I think the baptism of the Holy Spirit is amazing. If I can give one key or step to victory and success to someone who is trapped in some kind of bondage, and, honestly, we all have had something in our lives that is like a trap, it would be giving your life over to Jesus. Just let it go for Him; ask Him into your heart. The second key is to ask for the infilling of the Holy Spirit, with the evidence of speaking in tongues. It is powerful, and He is there to help you and to equip you to live victoriously. Just ask Him and He will come, and then you will receive. Don't think about it, just do it. The gospel of Luke 11:10-13 in *The Message* Bible states:

> Don't bargain with God. Be direct. Ask for what you need. This is not cat-and-mouse, hide-and-seek game we're in. If your little boy asks for a serving of fish, do you scare him with a live snake on his plate? If your little girl asks for an egg, do you trick her with a spider? As bad as you are, you wouldn't think of such a thing— you're at least decent to your own children. And don't you think the Father who conceived you in love will give the Holy Spirit when you ask Him?

God wants to give you all things richly to enjoy, and one of His many gifts is His presence with you, upon you, and in you. Oh, praise God!

The Bible is clear that Jesus is the same today, yesterday, and forever. If He had to have the Holy Spirit and His power, then we do too. This isn't about any church doctrine or whether you're Catholic, Baptist, or whatever. There are no denominations in heaven. We are all one worshipping God, and that is the way it should be here on earth. All the different denominations really are man-made. I thank God for the church of Jesus Christ, but what good is the church without power? We know the Holy Spirit is power.

God always knows what He is doing. He knows what we need even more than we do. I needed the gas in my car; I needed the Holy Spirit to help me in all my weaknesses. God knew the anguish and pain I was going to suffer while incarcerated, but He also knew the victories I would experience there. After all these years, I wouldn't change a thing because of what I have learned and how all those years of suffering helped me to see how valuable God is, how valuable I am, and how valuable life is in general.

As you've read earlier in this chapter, I was sentenced to two years in a Florida state facility. I am going to go ahead and tell you so you won't be wondering anymore about the miracle God gave me. I didn't have to do forty years in prison; the Lord was so merciful with me. After being sentenced to state time, the federal government came and got me after months in the state prison and took me to a county jail, which houses federal prisoners awaiting sentencing.

I was sentenced to two more years in a federal prison, so my entire time in prison would be three years with "gaintime," that is, time that I had already spent locked up, and six months in a halfway house to adjust myself to freedom again.

A few weeks after I was sentenced, the prison bus came to get me. For security reasons, they never tell you when you're going. But, it is usually very early, about four in the morning. This begins the process of taking you to your new location.

I remember the fear that I started to feel as the lights came on and my bunkies that were with me looked at me and said, "This is it, you are out of here!" I gave all my stuff away, except my Bible, as that was my lifeline.

I was escorted downstairs where I was turned over to state custody. They lined us up and put the handcuffs and the shackles on us. As we walked, we had to shuffle our feet to move. When we got onto the bus, we had to carefully lift our feet up. It was difficult because the chains only went so far. So, we pulled ourselves up onto the bus and sat two-by-two. The prison bus was an old, white school bus with wires and bars on the windows, and the entire bus was full of women going to the main induction prison in Florida. The journey on the bus would be about three or four hours.

The ride was something I will never forget. When we finally arrived at the reception center, I saw a prison for the first time in my life. I had been in a county jail—small, dirty and not as intimidating—but this prison was different. The first thing I noticed was all the armed guards waiting for the bus to arrive, then the huge gate attached to the fence that went for miles around this new address of mine. The fence had razor wire all over it. I remember girls in jail talking about how prison would be easier time and that it is better to go to prison. No time in jail or prison is easy, unless you are visiting as a church lady. In my case, I was a criminal doing my time, and I have to tell you I was really freaked out.

The inmates got off the bus and guards starting yelling for us to get in one straight line. They marched us into the facility then moved us into a building where we sat for hours as each one of us was called and given a new identity: our department of correction number. For the next three years, I would not be called by my name, at least not by the guards. I would be known as a number, and you better make sure you know your number. Then, the prison officials gave us dresses that we would wear as new inmates until orientation was over. If I remember right, that was about two weeks. During orientation, the prison does a complete examination of each person from top to bottom in order to determine if they would stay at the reception prison, as it was better equipped for people with medical needs, or, instead, if you would go off to a work camp where you planted trees. As for me, I went to the north facility for female prisoners in Gadsden.

Prison is a whole different culture. It is a city within itself, and there are state rules for running it. However, the inmates have their own rules. Not only did I need to learn about the prison rules, I had to learn about this new culture to which I was being introduced. I wasn't tough anymore; it was obvious. So, I spent a lot of time keeping to myself, and I clung to the Lord. As much as I could, I stayed in a state of constant prayer, either in my mind or in every private place I could find. I would stay in His Word at every waiting point. Now I knew why the Lord filled me with the Holy Spirit. I needed Him to make it through what I was experiencing.

I dreaded showers during orientation. We had ten minutes to take a shower. We went in running to get the first available one. There were about ten showers to pick from, but the worst ones were the two at the end. The guards were at one end in a round cubicle with glass. They would watch us and sometimes yell at us with the loud speakers from the shack, telling us that that our ten minutes were up or to stop ladies from having a confrontation with one another. I prayed that I would not get the end showers by the guard shack.

A set of ten showers was on the other side of the wall. So, when one group would come, the guard would watch the first ten, and then switch to the other side. It wasn't as bad if the guard was a female, but when the guard was a male, it was quite difficult. The first time, I got the shower by the guard shack; the guard on duty was a male. He expressed his delight in his free peep show. It was so painful for me that I didn't want to shower. After my first experience, the Lord helped me to avoid that shower and I didn't see that guard again in orientation.

Prayer works and I know that other ladies were praying for him not to return.

The next two weeks went by so slowly. In the mornings at about three-thirty, we were awakened by the screams of "Get up! Get out of bed!"

It was just like a boot camp that I had seen on TV, but this wasn't training to protect our country. Our country was being protected from us. After lining up at the door at about four in the morning so that we could be lead to the Chow Hall, we were instructed that there was to be no talking. If you talked, you were pulled from the line abruptly, yelled at, and then led away for punishment.

It was January and, in Florida, it can be cold. On one particular morning, it was freezing and I had no coat. They gave us coats when we first got there, but there were not enough for everyone, so I gave my coat to an older woman who was in line. The wind was blowing and I was freezing while waiting for the cafeteria to open their doors. Looking toward the sky, the heavens and the stars that I had not seen in over a year or more amazed and completely captivated me. I had never seen so many stars in my life, and now that I was saved, I saw the enormous creation of our God. I wanted to shout but couldn't. I looked at the stars like a blind person might when seeing for the first time. It was the most amazing thing I had ever seen in my life. Even through all the razor wire, God's beauty and His love was staring right back at me. He overwhelmed me with His presence right there in the cold winter morning. After that, nothing seemed to bother me—not even the showers.

After orientation was over, things got much easier, and I was able to spend a lot more time with the Lord and in church. Night and day, I would spend time reading the Word and praying. My first bunkie was an older woman who had been sentenced to life in prison. She taught me the ropes until I was moved to a new facility. I appreciated her helping me over that hump. I know that God placed me with her purposely to help me get adjusted.

After months, I was transferred to a facility in north Florida. If I thought the first place was bad, nothing could have prepared me for what this place was like. When our bus arrived, I could feel the evil around this place. It was almost like a gray cloud was over it. Adjusting here was not going to be easy. I was being overcome by evil instead of me overcoming evil with good.

The dorm I was in had over eighty women, lots of fighting and noise, and lights that never really turned off. I really thought I was going to lose my mind in this place. I wasn't prepared for this; I was sinking fast. I thought I might break mentally. I couldn't even function properly. I was praying so hard for God to remove me from this place. I didn't know how He could do it, but I pleaded desperately for Him to get me out of there. I deserved to be here for the crimes I had committed, but I didn't know how I would handle this. The one good thing about this place was the church service. It was a church on fire for God, and, oh, how I wished I could stay in church every day. Another thing that would keep me going was my mom and dad finally coming to visit me. After almost two years of not hugging my mom, I was about to do just that!

Finally, the day arrived for visitation. My name was called to go to the visitor's center where my mom and dad were waiting. I wore no make-up and had gained some weight, but I had long hair now. The biggest difference with me was the fact that I was saved and had Jesus in my life. When I came into the center, my mother jumped up from the table. I walked as quickly as I could toward her (without getting in trouble for it) and went straight into her open arms—wide open for me.

After we hugged for a long time, she stepped back and looked at me with great joy and said, "I can see Jesus all over you! You look like an angel!"

I found out later that after the visit, my mom contacted all our family on both sides and told them that I would never go back to my previous lifestyle, and I would never be the same again. I still have the letter she wrote to the family and I cherish it. She told my family that I looked like an angel coming through the door and that she saw Jesus all over me. Wow, what an awesome thing to say about me! That is the greatest compliment that anyone can get, especially for someone like me who used to look like the devil!

My mother had believed for eighteen years that God would save her daughter and He did. It just goes to show that you should never give up! God is faithful no matter what. He is faithful, and my mom was seeing the labor of all her tears and prayers fulfilled right before her eyes. She was correct in her judgment: I never went back. She didn't know then about the federal charges, and, at that time neither did I. But, that didn't seem to matter. She got her little girl back, and that was such a relief after all those years of torment that I put her through. She could breathe; she could finally relax. She knew with everything in her that I was changed and that God had a firm grip on me.

Chapter 11

Overcoming Evil

Iwas really struggling at the north facility in Gadsden where I was transferred. My reprieve from all the chaos around my newest location was the chapel. Walking the track around the facility, I was praying so hard for a miracle, that God would get me out of this place. I remember one day, as I was walking the track, a family of deer came out of the woods that was right beside us. These deer came directly to the fence and I stopped to watch them. I was amazed and thought to myself that it was weird that the deer, animals, were free and I was behind the fence. I told the Lord that something was really wrong with this picture.

It was as if the deer had gone on a family outing. The daddy deer, the mommy deer, and their children had come to the "people zoo" to look through the fence at the caged humans. Just like we do when we go to a petting zoo. Again, it reinforced that, with the Lord's help, I would never come back to a place like this again. If I did come back, it would be to preach the Gospel and to help others out of the darkness into God's Light.

One morning as I was doing my work detail, a guard came and told me I was to go back to my dorm and pack all my stuff because I was leaving. I was amazed. I had been asking God to remove me from this place, and a day or two after seeing my mom, the officials were telling me to pack up. As I walked back to the dorm, I thought, *Does this mean I get to go home or what, God?* I had asked Him to get me out of that place, and that is exactly what He did. I ran to the other dorm to see if my friend, the same friend who got saved with me, my former partner in crime, who now belonged to God. I went to say good-bye to her, but when I got to her dorm I found that she was packing to leave also.

I got all my stuff together and went to the reception center to be released. After they released my friend and me, two men came with badges and arrested us again on the federal charges. They placed handcuffs on us and put us in the back of a black SUV with government- issued plates. The windows were darkly tinted and they would not let us take any of our belongings with us. I begged the two officers to please at least let me take my Bible, and they agreed. Everything else stayed behind, but I had all I needed.

My friend and I asked the two officers where we were going, and they refused to tell us. We were in the SUV and away we went. It was so scary because not even the state facility knew where we were going, nor did my family. I was praying with my friend because we were freaked out. We had no idea who these men were and where they were taking us. After hours in the back of the car, we came to a jail. I don't remember where we were, but they rushed us in there. We couldn't have any contact with anyone but officers and trustees who were supervised by the guard to make sure we didn't speak with them. Still, we had no idea what was going on. All we could do was pray and trust God for His protection.

The night we spent in that jail was a night of no sleep. It was hard not to know what was happening and to feel so helpless. I had no control over what was happening. If they wanted to take us to another country they could. We were helpless and completely at their mercy.

As morning came, so did the two federal officers. Again, we were given no information. We were escorted quickly out of the jail and into the back of the black SUV, and we were off again. We went to the Tallahassee Federal Prison. When I saw the maximum-security facility, I was almost in a panic. At that time, the place looked like something from an Alfred Hitchcock movie. It was scary. I was thankful that I wasn't at the state facility, but it seemed like I went from the fire to the frying pan.

As we pulled up, the officers finally told us that we would not be staying there, but, instead, we were simply picking up two men from the facility who were going to where we were going. Little did I know that Tallahassee prison that instilled so much fear in me was going to be my new home in the very near future.

I asked again where we were going—again, no answer. They wanted us to tell all, but they told us nothing. I prayed, sang songs, and prayed some more. My friend was in tears, and I wanted to cry too, but I felt peace in my heart that everything was going to be all right. We just needed to hold each other up. As I was praying, I felt in my heart that two are better than one because they keep each other from falling. After that I was fine. I knew that God was with my friend and me, no matter what.

After what seemed like hours on the road, we arrived at our destination. While on the road, I was able to share the gospel with the men we picked up, so our time was not wasted. The Lord prevailed through it all. Finally, they told us what was going on. We were charged with the federal charges, and we would be held in this jail waiting to see the magistrate for sentencing.

I was happy to have this chapter of my life coming to an end. Now, I would find out how much longer I would be held behind bars. The Lord also answered my prayer by removing me from the prison I had been in. I was being overtaken by evil instead of me overtaking evil with good. He always gives us a way out of any temptation, and the last place I had been in was full of temptation.

I didn't realize it at the time, but God moved me to that jail for a purpose. He brought me there to become more in His Spirit, to provide strength for my upcoming years behind bars. Most of my state time was going to be completed at this jail. But, it was in jail that I was introduced to the ministry of Joyce Meyer. At this facility I started watching her on TV. God used her as a lifeline for me. Her ministry has been so instrumental in introducing to me to Jesus, the real Jesus. Through her, God gave me so much hope. She suffered sexual abuse as I did. Her abuse was at the hand of her father, and mine was at the hand of a neighbor. Nevertheless, she went through so much, and the Lord completely healed her. Now, He uses her to touch millions of people in her ministry. I thought to myself, *If He did that for Joyce, then He could do that for me.* Everyday, I watched her program. I started contacting her ministry to see if they would send me books, and they did. It was awesome! I had nothing to give to them, but they sent me books anyway. I was so blessed by that. I read those books over and over again.

Kenneth Copeland was another minister that helped me a lot. His ministry sent whatever they could to help me grow in the grace and knowledge of God. There are no words of gratitude I can use to effectively express how much of an impact they had on my life. Well, actually, yes I can! It is with the words in this book and how I am still standing with God today.

When I was taken back to prison, I actually became a partner of both ministries. I only had twenty dollars a month coming in, but I would always send one dollar to Joyce's ministry and one dollar to Kenneth Copeland. This was one way to pay my tithes to the Lord. God used them both to help me overcome all that I was facing.

I had lost my sister, and now I was looking again at a lot more time incarcerated, plus, I had just found out that my mother had been diagnosed with liver cancer in addition to her long-time condition of cirrhosis of the liver. Gloria Copeland taught me about healing, Kenneth and Brother Hagin taught me about faith, and Joyce taught me about the mind, all the bad heart conditions, wrong behaviors, and wrong thinking patterns I had accumulated.

I suffered a lot while incarcerated. I know that when one is in prison, it is to punish —and it does. Something is wrong if you don't see it as punishment. However, I did meet ladies for whom prison was a reprieve from their abusers. They would rather spend their time be-hind bars than to be beaten and abused by husbands, lovers, or family members.

Now that I am released, I look back and I ask myself, how much punishment is enough? Who sets that bar of punishment? I am not saying that people shouldn't pay for their crimes. There are always repercussions for bad choices. After all, you reap what you sow. But, honestly, when does someone finally pay back for their wrongs, how many times does someone have to prove themselves? How much suf-fering does someone have to go through before society says, "OK you are free now"? No wonder God says to forgive and that He forgives us. Because we can't pay the debt we owe, there is no way.

There are not enough ways to say you're sorry. There is not enough restitution to pay. People can't pay back society anymore after doing their time. Is it fair that after someone is released from prison they still have to pay for the mistakes they made by being labeled the rest of their life as an ex-offender? When is it enough?

Is it fair that this individual can't vote, can't get a job, and is refused from apartment complexes where they are trying to find a home? Some churches don't want people out of prison in their church. When is the punishment enough and when can someone be accepted as human again? These men and women behind bars are human beings, created in God's image, and they are valuable to Him. They are someone's father, mother, sister, brother, son, or daughter.

Not everyone is a bad apple. People do change; the way they change is with the Word of God. It's not just a book; it is a living text. The Bible is God Himself and His Words, and it produces life in an individual. If the gospel is not preached, how will they hear? And if they don't hear, there will be no change. Is prison ministry important? Yes, I think it is on the top of God's list to help prisoners, orphans, and widows. God even says in Hebrews 13:3 not to forget the prisoners and to think of yourself as one. What is He saying? Don't be too quick to erase them from existence, because God is also in that prison. Prisoners need the hand of God and His love so they can leave the darkness they're in. God said in Isaiah 45:3, "And I will give you the treasures of darkness." Have you ever thought that the people in bondage and behind bars are those hidden treasures?

After months being in the jail that housed federal prisoners, the Lord helped me and strengthened me. God was doing a lot of work in me. He healed my body from a terrible disease that caused me so much pain. He was healing my emotions. My mom was not doing well. So everything I learned about healing and faith I would share with her.

I was fighting hard in the spirit for my mom to be healed. The Lord healed her once for me, and He would do it again.

One time I called her and she was bleeding, hemorrhaging from the inside again, and was so sick that she couldn't even talk on the phone. I was praying fervently for her, and the Lord pressed me to contact a mentor from my hometown to ask her to go and anoint my mom with oil. The mentor agreed and the Lord healed my mom. She was up and running again!

Because of my mom being ill, I had written out a petition to God for my release on probation with the federal charges. That would be a big miracle, but, then again, we serve a big God. I wanted to get home to give back to my mom the love I withheld from her all those years when I was out on the streets. I wanted to comb her hair and go to the movies with her. I just wanted to love her and be with her. I found every scripture I could about being free and the opening of prison doors and wrote them out. I think it was a page and half. I presented this to the Lord before my court date so that He would move on the judge's heart to release me.

The court date finally arrived. This would tell me how much time I was going to get. I was taken to the federal courthouse in Orlando. I was in an SUV again, and we were taken into a basement. I was in a holding cell, and while I was there, I was praying and reading over the scriptures that I so diligently worked to put together. As I was pacing back and forth, the spirit of God came on me and His love consumed me. I stopped and said to Him as I tore up all those scriptures, "Lord, if I am not ready to get out, then not my will but Yours be done. If I am not ready, please don't let me out. I don't want to go back to the way I was."

The guard escorted me to the federal courtroom. My name was called, and I stood before the judge. I could not tell you what happened and what was said. It was like I was in a bubble. I felt God as these people determined my future. I knew that God was controlling every minute and every action on both sides.

The judged looked at me and then said, "I sentence you to two years in federal prison."

I said thank you to her, and she looked greatly surprised that I would say thank you, and then I thanked the Lord. In total, as I mentioned previously, I did three years in prison when it could have been forty years. Truly, the three years with six months in a federal halfway house was a Bible school and complete training and breaking for me. I wasn't going to be with my mom yet, but I trusted God to keep her healed and that I would be with her again. It was better than if I were free to go home and get messed up again.

The remaining year and a half that I was incarcerated was the worst and some of the hardest times I have ever experienced. But, it was also the best thing that could ever happen to me. Why? Because I found out that God is with me and He will never leave me. He helped me through so much. There is not enough time to share everything in this book, but it is amazing how He brought me through so much pain, depression, loneliness, and fear.

The federal sentencing was over, and back to the Gadsden I went. But, this time, it was different for me because "greater is He who is in me, than he who is in the world" (1 John 4:4). I came back like the lion of Judah. I came back preaching and full of the spirit of God. This time the evil didn't overtake me, but with the Lord's help I overcame evil, plus, on top of that, I got to hug my mom again!

Chapter 12

Halfway Done

My state prison time was over. I had reached the halfway point with my three-year sentence. Still, I learned from the Lord not to count the days, that each day was a gift and to stay in each one. I couldn't look to the future because it was too painful, too uncertain. It made me become very impatient. You need a lot of diligence, endurance, and patience in prison. But, to be honest, you need these attributes as a Christian as well, and I was in training for the real world.

I was moved to a county jail to wait for the federal prison officials to come and get me. I had no idea where I was, just somewhere in Florida. They only let me have a Bible—and I had to beg for that! For the time I was in prison, I could be outside, smell the fresh air, and feel the sun on my face. That was not the case in this jail, and they escorted me to an isolation cell.

When I was just starting out, that was fine for me. I had just gotten saved and that was a safe haven for me, a cocoon. But now an isolation cell was more like a tomb. I was completely alone. I had no belongings. At times they even forgot I was in that cell. This was the loneliest period of time I have ever experienced in prison. When I say belongings, I mean, basic necessities like soap, shampoo, comb, toothbrush, deodorant, and toothpaste. I had *none* of these things.

My cell was filthy. At least it had a private shower. But, just cold water; that was all. I was fed through an open slat in the door. After I got my food, it was shut tight. This was a challenge, again, because I wasn't able to walk or even see the outside, or see my mom or talk with her. There was no church either. I didn't know how long I would be there and that greatly concerned me.

Before writing this book, I wondered how much I should share about my incarceration. But, I think it's important to show that no matter what you go through, God will see you through. He is able to reach down and help anyone. Jesus is not just in church, nor does He only come around on Sundays and mid-week services. He is there all the time. He is in you, upon you, and around you.

Also, I wanted to share that He goes into the byways and the prisons and into the lowest parts to help and retrieve His children. If you cry, He will be there and He will hear you. He reached down for Joseph, who was in prison. He reached down to Daniel, who was in a lion's den. He reached down to Jeremiah, who was in a dungeon. And He reached down to Paul and Silas, who were in prison. He also reached down to a prisoner named Teresa. I had been guilty before, but not anymore. Jesus took my guilt and shame.

I know what it feels like to be completely alone. I know what it feels like to be despised and rejected. I know what it feels like to be looked upon as an animal or someone so disgusting that people are afraid they might catch something from you. I know what it is like to not know where your next meal is coming from. But you know what? Jesus knows those things also. He went through it all. This enables Him to understand and comfort us and help us. That's what He did with me after that isolation cell locked shut. Hearing that steel door shut behind me was like the closing a coffin with me in it.

It was the third day, and I had no way of washing my hair. When you are incarcerated, there is no way to do your hair. So, during the year, my hair had grown midway down my back. It was the longest it had ever been. I used a tiny bar of soap, like what you get in the hotel in order to try to wash my hair, which made all kinds of tangles in it. I had no comb except for a portion of a broken comb I found on the floor of the cell. It had about four teeth in it, but I was thankful for it, and I began to try to comb my hair. The jail did provide me with a little tube of toothpaste and a toothbrush that fell apart in my mouth as I brushed my teeth. I actually was brushing my teeth with my finger. I was beginning to smell and I began to pray. I said, "Father, I know that you don't want your child smelling and looking like this, so I need your help! I ask You Lord for shampoo, a comb, deodorant, and a real toothbrush and toothpaste."

Keep in mind that I was in isolation. I had no one around me except the guards, and they are not allowed to give the inmates anything. I started praying and worshipping the Lord and worked on combing my hair with my four-tooth comb. I kept thanking Him for everything I could think of, and then finally it was time to go to bed.

In the morning when I awoke, I heard the trap door open to my cell door. When I looked there was a new stick of deodorant, a big comb with all its teeth, a real toothbrush and toothpaste, and a big bar of soap. I started praising God so much. I don't know who did it, but I know it had to be a guard because no one even knew I was there except the guards. I don't know who God used—maybe it was an angel sent by God—all I know is that I got my hair combed and I didn't smell anymore. All I needed now was the shampoo, and God arranged for that also.

Later that day, as I was reading my Bible and praying, I could hear a girl cussing and yelling. Then, I heard the guard telling her to be quiet. All of the sudden the cell opened and in came a young girl who also was an inmate. She was fighting mad! She had just beaten up a girl in population and she was fired up.

I was thinking to myself, *Great, this girl is going to try to fight with me now*, and with the language this girl was using, she was clearly upset.

I just kept reading and praying under my breath and taking authority over the devil. Then, all of the sudden, she just stopped, turned and looked at me, and said, "Hey, who are you and where did you come from?"

I explained that I was waiting to go to the federal prison and that I was in state prison prior to coming to this jail. She looked around and said, "Are you OK?"

I told her I was just fine and we began to talk. She told me that she was in the other portion of the jail and got in a fight with another girl, and they had moved her into my cell to calm her down before they took her back to general population. So, I started to share with her about the Lord and how He loved her. I asked her if she would like to receive Him as her Lord and Savior. Honestly, after all these years, I can't remember if she did receive Jesus. I don't think she did, but God used her to bring my shampoo and conditioner. She asked me if I needed anything, and I told her shampoo would be great.

She said, "I will have the nurse bring you some tonight." That night the trap door opened, and I had so much stuff that when I left to go to federal prison, I left the comb and everything that God blessed me with so that the next lady who had that cell would not have to go through what I did. Though it may not seem like much, He proved again to me how He was with me and that He was concerned about everything that concerned me.

Maybe this chapter should be called the miracle chapter. Since I have been with the Lord, He has performed miracle after miracle. My entire life, since giving my heart to the Lord, has been one challenge after another challenge, but with all the challenges have come answered prayers. His Hand has provided for every need, and He has encouraged and uplifted me every time. Psalms 68:5–6 in the *God's Word* translation states, "The God who is in His holy dwelling places is the father of the fatherless and the defender of widows. God places lonely people in families. He leads prisoners out of prison into productive lives, but rebellious people must live an unproductive land."

I was finally moved, after months of not breathing fresh air, feeling the wind on my face, seeing the sun and birds, or running my toes through the grass. When they came and got me, I didn't care where they took me, just so long as I was getting out of this terrible place. As we went down the road, I saw signs that read "Tallahassee." I knew where I was going! I was going to the Alfred Hitchcock prison. This was my new address for a year and a half, and it would be that year and a half that would either make me or break me, and, fortunately, my stay did both.

After all the processing and procedures were completed, I received my new bunk and started learning all the rules for this prison. The guards were different here, as were most of the ladies housed here. I was definitely in a maximum-security prison. There seemed to be more respect from the guards to the inmates and vice versa. My charges of theft and credit card fraud didn't warrant me being in maximum-security, but the Lord was keeping me separated from my friend now.

I'm sure you remember my former partner in crime, who was arrested with me. Well, we might have gotten saved together, but that didn't mean we were both headed in the same direction. I was heading full speed into God, and my friend was slipping back into her old ways and behaviors. Letting go of our friendship was hard for me. It is not something I wanted to do, but it is something that God was requiring from me. So, with His help I did. Was it painful? Yes. But was it worth it? Yes, it was. If you want to become a winner, then you need to hang around other winners. For me, at the time, my winners were the Father, Son, and Holy Spirit.

I had prayed before coming to this prison to get a work detail where I could learn how to grow a garden. Obviously, during my old life of addiction, I didn't appreciate the outdoors or all the beauty around me. I thought it would be cool to work outside since I was locked up without fresh air for so long. God answered my prayer and put me in the Horticulture Department where the first thing we learned was how to grow a garden.

It was there that the Lord gave me a release from the pressures of the prison, and He helped me understand about breaking our stubborn will and dying to our ways. The Lord also taught me about hard work. In my old life, I would stay up all night partying or stealing, whatever the night held, and then come home to sleep all day. Who could keep a job? I was incredibly lazy and extremely stingy before coming to Jesus. But, when God got a hold of me, I always gave everything away. I worked hard planting plants, mowing grass, and doing anything I could and always went above the call of duty.

I had purposed in my heart before coming into this place that the way I went into prison was not the way I was coming out. I wanted desperately to be changed inside and out. One of the first things God did was begin teaching me to be a hard worker and to follow the rules. So, I started working in the rain, cold, and heat without a complaint or care. They simply let me work!

The prison facility had many flowerbeds. My job was to grow different flowers with the seeds, and then, after they matured enough to be planted, I would design the beds with these flowers. This job became such a lesson to me about dying and growing. Of course, I don't mean dying physically. I mean exchanging your way of doing things for God's way, dying to yourself and dying to your will. Truly, that is repentance. This is the process of being a Christian, daily exchanging your junk for God's excellence and glory.

I had many petunia seeds that I would take from the plants already grown. Instead of throwing them away after trimming the flowers, I would take them to the greenhouse. They were bright green, pod-looking things with hundreds of little seeds inside. The problem with them was that they did me no good; they produced no life until they died.

Many people in the world and in churches believe that drug addiction is a disease. In fact, a long time ago, some medical books even claimed that homosexuality was a disease. This is not the case. Sin is a choice. Sin is a disease, but it's a disease of the soul. It is the fallen nature of the person, not their original intent. Every choice we make throughout our lives produces life or death; there is no way around it. Until we die to the choices that lead to death, we will not truly live. In my life, I didn't realize how in the dark I was until the light was turned on. I can tell you I have lived what I thought was living. But, it was death and it produced addiction, shame, and sexual perversion.

Drug addiction, homosexuality, theft, lying, and judging others are all choices. We choose what we want. We have a choice, and we don't have to allow those sins to have power over us. We choose what we think. It was such a revelation to me when I found out that I had a choice of what I let in my head. There is so much freedom in knowing that I can choose what I think, how I feel, and what I do. This is why you will never hear me say I am an addict or in recovery. I am not.

When I chose to give my heart to the lordship of Jesus Christ, I chose right then and there that my old life of addiction, homosexuality, stealing was over. Because of the choice He made when He died on the cross, because of His death and resurrection, He made a way for me to choose death and a resurrection also. I died to the addiction and was resurrected to a new life of freedom. "Once an addict always an addict" is not true. It is a lie! I am proof of that. There is power and life in the Word of God.

The Bible clearly says that when Jesus sets you free, you are free indeed. If anyone is in Christ, he is new creation, a whole new species altogether. Plus, the Bible gives us a list in Psalms 103 of all the benefits that God has. Being in Christ, being His child makes these benefits available to you. So if you still believe that addiction is a disease after reading all His benefits, then God has healed you already because He heals all diseases. That is one of His many benefits. So what does this have to do with seeds and planting? I am about to tell you.

After I dried those petunia seeds and let them die, I was amazed. They didn't look like anything. I had to secure them in a box so the wind wouldn't take them away. They were brown and dead, no life in them it seemed—until I planted them. Weeks passed and I would see a tiny shoot pop up and then there would be a leaf. One day, they were mature enough to go to the flowerbed to be planted, where they eventually became some of the prettiest flowers I had ever seen, and the whole facility, even God, could enjoy them.

Christianity is about dying to your old choices and being resurrected to God's choices. There is always pain in dying, and there is sorrow. Not all people are comfortable giving up, but the reward is great when you do. When I gave up my friendship with my old partner in crime, God gave me friends all over the world. You find a freedom that you have never experienced in your life. Death is freeing; you are released from this world.

Look at a caterpillar; it dies, but in its death it becomes a butterfly. It is free to move wherever the wind blows it. Before, it was limited to the dirt and the ground level of things where it could crawl. When we continue in the wrong choices, we limit ourselves to the ground level when God wants to take us to the penthouse. Going up, anyone?

Think about this: when a person dies, the physical body decomposes, but through the death of the body, which is like the seed, the soul and spirit of that person is then free to be what they are supposed to be.

The Bible is clear in John 12:24 (KJV) that "Unless the grain of wheat falls into the ground and dies, it abides alone, but if it dies, it bears much fruit." The Amplified Bible states, "I assure you, most solemnly I tell you, unless a grain of wheat falls into the earth and dies, it remains [just one grain; it never becomes more but lives] by itself alone. But if it dies, it produces many others and yields a rich harvest." What is the rich harvest? You start doing things differently and you start being like God.

Honestly, the grain has life no matter what. It's alive, but it has an outer shell, like the petunia plant, encased in a green pod. But when you break that pod open that is where the rich harvest is, just like the outer shell on the grain. When it's broken, then the grain grows, and with that growth comes a harvest. When you eat an orange, you have to peel the outer skin to get to the good fruit. Then, you have the fruit, but the harvest isn't in the orange you just ate. It's the seeds of the orange that most of us spit out on the ground. But, what happens to those seeds? I am from Florida, and I have seen what happens to those orange seeds when they go into the ground and die. They become a whole orange grove!

I had a tough outer shell. My outer shell was my old life; you saw where that got me and what kind of life it produced. I remained inside myself, isolated in my own prison of wrong choices. The inner life is the Lord's new nature, which He placed inside me, and then the battle started because my hard outer shell didn't want to give Him a way inside. Similarly, if I don't peel the orange, then I can't eat the fruit, and both the seeds and fruit will rot. The inner life is the eternal life. If you don't allow the Spirit of God to do a work in and through you, then the inner life, the real life that is in you, will never be released. You must die before you can be resurrected.

Does this happen overnight? Heavens no! I am still finding things that I have to let die in my life so that the life of God can come out, even after seventeen years. I embrace the dying times now because I have experienced the benefits of the process. Believe me, it's so much better on the winning side. It's so much better becoming an orange grove then being a rotten orange, which is of no use to anyone—including me.

Every day in prison as well as after I was released has been about choices. The rest of my life will be about choices. I even had to choose to write this book. I didn't want to at first. I had many excuses why I couldn't.

First my computer broke down. Then, God brought the money for a new one. Then, I asked God for a quiet place to write, like maybe a place in the mountains. Not really thinking He would do it. Then, a lady at my church offered me the use of her cabin in North Carolina. I didn't ask—she came up on her own free will and told me she was sowing that into my life and then encouraged me to write the book. I said I didn't have the finances to go, and God brought the money for the gas and food. I fought God all the way, and then I finally died to my will and way. Now, I believe God will use this book for His Glory, and it will produce a harvest by helping others to know that you can make it.

I heard a story about the captain of a warship, who, on a foggy night, saw a light heading directly toward him, moving full speed ahead. In an attempt to stop both ships from colliding, the captain of the warship radioed the other ship's captain. He told the approaching ship to change course. The other ship declined and kept approaching full speed ahead. After the fourth request, the captain of the warship became aggressive and told the other ship to change course or else! The other ship radioed back and said, "No! You turn your ship ten degrees to the north. I am the lighthouse!" So many times we try to get God to conform to our ways of doing things, which will cause us to crash into rocks and sink our ship. Our victory and success comes by conforming to God's ways of doing things. He knows best and He knows what we need before we even ask Him.

We must understand that we don't make God conform to us. We want to be our own captain of our ship, but, unless we change course, we will run aground, sink our ship, and destroy everyone around us.. Honestly, we can't steer our own ship anymore. There are too many people drowning in the world that need you, and, believe it or not, God needs you. Let Him have the helm; let Him steer you through the fog. The fog does lift and there is always smooth sailing ahead, especially when He is steering the boat.

According to 2 Corinthians 4:6-12,

For God Who said, Let light shine out of darkness, has shone in our hearts so as [to beam forth] the Light for the illumination of the knowledge of the majesty *and* glory of God [as it is manifest in the Person and is revealed] in the face of *Jesus* Christ (the Messiah). However, we possess this precious treasure [the divine Light of the Gospel] in [frail, human] vessels of earth, that the grandeur *and* exceeding greatness of the power may be shown to be from God and not from ourselves. We are hedged in (pressed) on every side [troubled and oppressed in every way], but not cramped or crushed; we suffer embarrassments *and* are perplexed *and* unable to find a way out, but not driven to despair; We are pursued (persecuted and hard driven), but not deserted [to stand alone]; we are struck down to the ground, but never struck out *and* destroyed; Always carrying about in the body the liability *and* exposure to the same putting to death that *the Lord* Jesus suffered, so that the [resurrection] life of Jesus also may be shown forth by *and* in our bodies. For we who live are constantly [experiencing] being handed over to death for Jesus's sake that the [resurrection] life of Jesus also might be evidenced through our flesh which is liable to death. Thus death is actively at work in us, but [it's is in order that our] life [may be actively at work] in you.

Chapter 13

Mom

There is no greater disappointment than to believe in God for something and not get it. Maybe, I should say not get it the way you planned. There is a God-side to things and a man-side to things. Without man's cooperation with the God-side of things and His will, there isn't much God can do about it.

I like that about God the most. He didn't just make a bunch of robots to follow Him around and love Him on demand. I wouldn't want someone in my life that was forced to be with me. I had that kind of thing in my old life, and that is not love. If we are like this, not wanting a forced relationship, then what makes us think that God wants a forced relationship with us? He doesn't. That is why He gave each one of us freewill and free choices. He wants you to choose life and Him, but He won't force you to take what He provides through His Son.

This is similar to healing; for instance, Jesus paid the price on the cross, and *by His stripes we were healed.* Jesus took our sickness on the cross for us so that we can walk in divine health. I believe that with all my heart because I am proof of that firsthand, and so was my mother.

I was coming to end of my stay in federal prison. The three-year journey was almost over. The time did pass quickly, and I used every opportunity to become better acquainted with the Bible and with the Lord. Every morning He was the first person I went to. Then after my private time with the Lord, I would climb to the top of my bunk and put my headset on to watch Joyce Meyer's teachings every morning on the TV. God again used her to be a lifeline for me. The last year of my prison sentence was the most difficult, and I needed all The Word I could get. I hung on for dear life to whatever God used to heal, restore, and encourage me in this last phase of the journey.

Even on Saturdays, early in the morning I would get ready and go directly to the chapel where I would wait in the stairwell with patience and expectations, to see the chaplain coming through the courtyard. I was making sure she knew that I would be the first in line for the TV/video player in her office. It was there that I would spend hours watching teaching tapes from Joyce Meyer's ministry. Oh, how desperate I was for the comfort of God and His Word!

The last visit I had with my mother was heartbreaking. Prior to her coming, I received a letter from her. She stated that she was in a prison too and that she couldn't wait to have her little girl back home with her. But the good thing about what God did for both of us was that Mom was able to see her eighteen-year prayer answered when God set me free that July morning in 1997.

She wrote in one of her letters: "Lord, thank you for listening to my prayers. I waited patiently for the answer and it came." In this particular letter that arrived before her visit, she told me how she couldn't wait to see me. I believe it was October 21st.

Mom, as I look back now, was trying to prepare me for the struggle she was having with this sickness, but I wouldn't believe any report except the report of the Lord and what the Word said. She even asked me in one of her letters to not preach to her anymore, that she just wanted to talk mother-to-daughter. I was fighting hard for my mother's healing and shared everything I was learning about healing and the walk of faith with her. I knew I went overboard, but I was desperate to keep her alive.

This letter, in particular, touched my heart. She wrote, "When I first saw you Sunday at visitation you looked like a beautiful angel. Your faced gleamed; it shined like an angel had touched you. I know God changed you from a fallen angel into the one He knew you could be." Mom went on to say, "Do you know who I see each time I come to see you? I see my sweet little girl with golden hair, blue eyes, and a wonderful smile. I blow up with love." It was after these statements that she told me she didn't know exactly what was wrong, but she knew something was terribly wrong with her, and she was correct. She went on to tell me she didn't want to make me sad, but she didn't know if she was going to be alive much longer. She didn't know if she could hold out until I was released.

My sister died three days after I got saved, and then my mother became very ill, but the Lord healed her twice. When I came to the visitation center and saw her, it took my breath away. She was weak and her face was sunken in. My mother was a very pretty woman. She always reminded me of Doris Day. She was gorgeous. But, that day, I could tell she was very sick.

When I hugged her she winced in pain. As we talked, she told me that in addition to the cirrhosis of the liver, she had liver cancer. They told her she was dying and would be dying soon. I wouldn't believe that. I was not going to lose her to any sickness. I had caused so much pain in her life, and the fight had begun. It was probably selfish on my part, but I wanted to make up to her all those years that were destroyed in our relationship. She was doing her best to tell me she was going to be with the Lord, but I wouldn't believe it. I preached to her and told her what the Word said and that we had to stand on the Word—and that was final.

When my mom left me that day, I wanted to be angry, but instead I went deeper into God. I was afraid that if I let my emotions go wild that it would actually make matters worse for my mom. I had this idea that if I didn't walk a very strict line with God and lived completely obedient to His Word, then she wouldn't be healed. I didn't understand that God is full of grace, love, and mercy. It's not about us but about His Word and His sacrifice. Nevertheless, I walked a very rigid line. I began fasting, praying, and fasting some more. I was fighting hard with God, myself, and the devil, but I was determined to see my mom healed and ready to spend lots of time with her once I got out of prison to make up for all the time I had wasted.

I was hurting so deeply inside, but I just knew with all my heart that God would heal her—that actually He had already healed her. I needed God so badly to make it through this. Again, I wouldn't trade this time for anything because of the wonderful things He did for me in the last six months of my prison stay. He continued to show me that He was with me, giving me little signs along the way, demonstrating how mom and I were both in the palms of His hands.

I would be praying outside in the garden, and as I was praying, He would send a hummingbird over to me that would just hover right in front of me. Once, this bird literally sat on a branch right beside me while I prayed in the Holy Spirit. It was like that little bird knew what God was saying through me. On the way to work detail with my wheelbarrow in hand, early in the morning, I saw a big eagle perched upon a pole. It seemed to just stare right at me. I was amazed because there shouldn't have been any eagles around this place. Since that day, God encourages me often by sending me eagles in the most unusual places, just to let me know, "Hey Teresa, I am still with you."

As my time wound down to the last month or so, my mother was getting weaker. Oh, how I wanted to be with her, but that wasn't possible! I had to trust God.

One day after talking with mom on the phone, I couldn't wait to get out of the dorm and go walk on the track to blow off the steam of the hurt and pain I felt inside. I was terrified about the possibility of losing her even though I said nothing. She was so weak on the phone that she had to get off because she was too sick.

In prison there are certain times when you are counted. In those times, every inmate must be sitting on their bunks, the courtyard is closed. During count there is no movement in or out of dorms and everyone is quiet and must remain on each individual bunk until the prison officials give the all clear.

The minute count was over, and as soon as the doors were opened, I ran through the courtyard and up the hill until I finally got away by myself. I was crying so hard as I walked the track. I wasn't jogging, but my pace was close enough to jogging. I listened to a great gospel station in Tallahassee, and it was also a lifeline for me. I can't tell you what song was playing, but I knew it was God talking to me. The song kept saying He was there, and as I walked and cried I felt the presence of God come all around me. It was just Him and me on that track. For the first time, I saw Him as Father. It was like I had an open vision while I walked that track, and I could see His huge hand reaching toward mine. ·

My mother used to dress me up for church when I was a little girl. I was only four or five years old. I had lacy socks with black patent shoes and a pink and white dress with the back of the dress full of ruffles—the kind that bounce when you walk. As the Father's big hand reached down to my little hand, I could see me in that dress and Him holding my little hand as He walked His little girl all around that track. I literally walked with one arm up in the air for a couple of laps. I didn't care. I was being touched by my Father, and after that I could face with strength what was ahead of me, and thanks to Him I did.

I have to share one more miracle. The whole time I was in the federal prison, I received twenty dollars a month. I would send Joyce Meyer Ministries one dollar and Kenneth Copeland Ministries one dollar as well. This was my tithe. I believed the Word of God about giving and tithing, so if anyone would ask me for any coffee (which was like gold in prison) or anything else, if I had it, I gave it away. I am not sharing that to boast about myself. It's to show how you can't "out-give" God. He is faithful.

As I had no more money coming in, things were getting tight. My shampoo was to the point that I couldn't water it down anymore. I couldn't get any more soap out of the bottle if I tried. I had no more stamps. Everything was used up; I had nothing coming in. I had one more cup of coffee left, and a girl came by and asked me if I had any coffee. So, that was it—no coffee—she got the last cup.

As I was reading on my bunk one day, a girl from the other side of the dorm came over to my bunk. She and I would see each other in the morning while watching Joyce on TV and wave at each other across the warehouse of women. I called the dorm that because it was a huge building, as it housed about 80 to 100 beds that were filled by women.

This lady asked me to come over to her cubicle because she wanted to talk with me privately, so I agreed. As I climbed off my bunk to head over for the visit, my bunkie looked at me with a "what in the world is going on" expression. As I came to the lady's space, she told me to sit down, that her bunkie was gone, and that she had something she wanted to show me. Well, I started wondering what all the slinking around was about. She started to tell me that she was blessed with some money in her account. It was a lot more than she could even imagine. She was praying and asking God who she should tithe to or give an offering to and the Lord told her that I needed it.

I looked at her with amazement as she told me to reach under her bed to pull out a bag. It was a laundry bag and it was full. I could hardly lift it off the ground. It had two of everything that I used, and, as an added benefit, she had bought me a mango sherbet/ice cream they sold at the commissary that I liked a lot. God told her exactly what to buy.

Everything that was in that bag was what I normally used, but she didn't know that, and, yes, two containers of coffee with creamer were in that bag. The laundry bag was so full that I had to drag it back to my cubicle. I had to store some of it in my bunkie's locker because it all couldn't fit in mine. The lady told me that the only thing she asked was that I didn't tell anyone who did that for me, and I didn't. But I did tell everyone that it was God, because it was—that bag and all that was in it lasted me until the day I left. How amazing our God is!

The closer I got to my "out date," the harder it was for me being locked up. With only two weeks to go I was close to completing a little over three years behind bars. Now time seemed to stand still. The days grew long, and it seemed like every mean lady in that prison wanted to fight with me. I had no interest in fighting and I wasn't going to fight. By this point, nobody, including the devil, was going to keep me from leaving this place. It seemed as though all the stops were being pulled out by the enemy. I felt this was done in order to discourage me and to get me to make a wrong choice that would delay my freedom.

I was just getting ready to go outside and walk the track when a guard came and got me. The guard told me that I needed to see the classification officer for my release. The meeting wasn't just about my release. It was an emergency phone call from my dad saying that my mom was dying. She was in the hospital and this was it. Her liver had completely stopped functioning. All the blood in her body was backing up into her system. He told me that there was no hope of recovery.

I had two weeks left. Why now?

I got off the phone and told the classification officer what had happen and asked her if there was any way I could get an emergency release early just to be with my mom. She basically told me that it was my fault that my mom was dying that it was my choices that led me to this point, so I would just have to pay for it. I would not be able to go to her, and that was it. She was extremely cruel in her comments, but I held my tongue and said, "Yes, Ma'am." When I walked out of her office, I went directly back to my bunk and somehow found the strength to climb up to the top bunk. Immediately it was like being inside a bubble. The other 100 women were completely drowned out in my mind.

It was like everything was outside and I was inside this little bubble. I call it a bubble of grace. I started praying like I have never prayed before. I prayed so fervently in the Spirit that it was almost like groaning. It was a prayer for my mom's life. As I prayed, the tears streamed down my face and pain shuttered through my whole body. After three years of believing that my mom would be healed, now that I was almost released, she was slipping away. No, this just couldn't be!

I would not stop fighting. I was like a bulldog and there was no way I was letting go of her.

I could be nice to her now, and this was supposed to be a new start to our relationship. I could receive her love now and love her back the way I was supposed to love my mom. I was so close to finally treating her nicely and with respect. We had movies to see and places to go together. I had to laugh with her and play golf with her, and just be the daughter that she longed for me to be. It could not happen now, not this!

As I prayed, the presence of the Lord Himself came to me. I don't know if you know what I mean by that. But, it was a different presence than usual. It was Jesus Himself and I knew it. I immediately stopped praying. I knew it was over.

That is when I asked Him, "She is going with you isn't she?" and He answered me with the sweetest voice I have ever heard. He was so loving and kind to me.

And, very gently, He answered, "Yes."

A great peace came to me and my tears stopped. I asked Him if it was at all possible, since I made her suffer so much in this life, that He could help her not to suffer so much in her dying. He didn't answer me on that, but there was such a bubble of grace that came upon me, His presence was thick on me and it stayed that way for a long time. I told Him it was OK now. I let her go. I wouldn't fight Him anymore.

After the Lord came to me, I climbed down off my bunk and I went to the chapel. The chaplain had just found out and asked me if I would like to phone my mother to see if possibly she was able to speak to me. I said please, yes. As she dialed the phone, I was trying to figure out what to say. This could be the last time I talk with my mom. What are the words that I wanted to say? There was so much to say, but what are the right things? A slew of emotions raged through my mind and body, but I had to keep my cool for my mom's sake.

I asked the Lord, "OK, if Mom is going with You, please help me to glorify You through this whole thing. I can't do this myself, and I just want people to see Your hand on me and that You would be glorified through this whole experience."

The chaplain handed me the phone. I didn't know for sure, who was on the line, but I heard her.

I said, "Mom" and she said, "Hi, Sweetheart, I am sorry I am not going to be here for you." I told her I knew and that it was OK, she could go now. She was so excited to hear me say that.

She replied "thank you," like a little kid. I was holding her back from going on. I really fought hard for her and through my prayers and determination I was giving God not one bit of any slack. He had to do this for me, even if that is not what my mom wanted. It wasn't. She was tired and now my acceptance released her. She was free without the worry of me. She got to see what the Lord did for me, and she knew I was going to be OK. I told her not to wait for me, to just let God do what He needed to do.

I asked her if she was scared and she told me, "Heavens no. I finally get to see what my Heavenly Father looks like and what He has prepared for me." I asked her to please say hello to Jackie for me, that I would be with them real soon, and that I was so sorry for all the problems I had caused them. As I hung up the phone, it seemed that would be the last time I would hear my mom's voice.

Eventually, the years behind bars finally came to an end for me. The last two weeks of my stretch were a blur. I just remember it wasn't me. It was the Lord carrying me through. I was in a God bubble or a grace bubble. As they gave me my release papers, I was instructed that a taxicab would be waiting for me outside to take me to the nearest bus station. A bus would take me to Tampa to a halfway house located behind a Goodwill store. I had no idea where I was going, but I followed the few instructions they gave me. I had six months in a halfway house to help me adjust to the outside world again. Leaving the prison was bittersweet for me. I was happy to finally be free, but my parents weren't there to pick me up as planned. My mom was on her deathbed and still holding on.

With a little money and one pair of jeans and a T-shirt, I walked away from the large concrete walls with razor wire and armed guards, never to return again. I entered the cab that drove me to the bus station. I was freaked out by the busyness of everything. Prison is another world entirely, and things run slowly, not at a fast pace. Now, people were zooming by in such a hurry that I became overwhelmed, plus I didn't know how to purchase a ticket for a bus ride. It had been years since I had ridden a bus! The taxi driver helped me. With the hundred dollars they gave me, I purchased my ticket; I paid the taxi cab driver, and then bought myself a Coke. I had no luggage, just a radio for gospel music and, of course, my Bible.

It was late in the morning before I arrived at the Tampa bus station, which was downtown. I took a cab to the halfway house. I was still prison property, but it was different now: no walls. When I arrived, the only thing I could think of was getting to my mother. The next day, I went to the counselor who was assigned to me and asked if they would allow me to go see my mother. I explained to her that she was dying and that I just needed to see her. It had been three years. Please let me say good-bye and hug her. I told them about my brother, who was in the Air Force. He was here, and I asked them if they would give me a furlough if he agreed to come and get me and escort me to my mother and then bring me back? Praise God, they agreed! The next day they let me come home for eight hours. After over three years, I was coming home, but I was coming home to my mom on her deathbed.

As I walked in the house, my aunt announced to my mom that I was there. My mother was in a kind of coma that she would go in and out of. She moaned loudly, and shook her head back and forth, like don't mess with me about that, as if she was waiting for me. Then, I walked into her room. My mother sat upright to the best of her ability, gasped with excitement when she saw me, and then slumped over. She basically took her last waking breath after seeing me. She slipped into a coma for certain after that. I went to hug her, but I couldn't as she was in a fetal position. I did get to kiss her forehead and told her she was a little stinker for waiting for me. I had told her not to do that, but she wanted one last glimpse of her little girl. This time, her little girl was back and better than she had ever been. The presence of the Lord was strong in the room as I read to her the rest of the time I had with her. I read from John 14:1-3 (KJV): "Let not your heart be troubled: ye believe in God, believe also in Me. In my Father's house are many mansions: if it were not so, I would have told you. I go to prepare a place for you. And if I go and prepare a place for you, I will come again, and receive you unto myself; that where I am, there ye may be also."

After an hour or so with my mom, I had to return to the halfway house, but I was thankful that I got to see her and she got to see me one last time. My mother died three days after I was released from prison, just one day after I visited her. My family called the counselor at the halfway house to tell me that my mother had left to go to her mansion-in-heaven with my sister. I recently found out that when Mom went to heaven, my sister Jackie was waiting for her. My aunt told me that when Mom went to be with the Lord, as she was taking her last breath, she saw Jackie and said her name. My mom got to see her oldest daughter. Jackie was the one who greeted her into heaven.

There is no greater disappointment I could have experienced than this. I waited and believed for three years that I would be with her, but that wasn't in the plan. Did God heal her? Yes, He did. Did God fail me? No, He didn't. My prayer for her healing was just answered differently than I expected. It wasn't what my mother wanted. She wanted to be with the Lord and see Jackie. She missed her a lot.

While I was at my parent's house visiting my mom, I was amazed at what she had done for me before she got really sick. I went into my bedroom and found that she had all my clothes packed for me. On top of my clothes was a letter she wrote to me and something that was so important to me, my baby picture that she had torn in half. She tore my baby picture in half and told me to never come back, that I wasn't welcomed here anymore. Her daughter was welcome, but not the person I had become. On top of the clothes along with the letter was my baby picture taped back together and framed. She knew that one day I would return, and I did. I keep that picture of me on my desk to remind me of the restoration of God and how far He has brought me over the years. Mom was so sweet. She didn't tear into my face in the photo, just the bottom half of me—not my face. I think she didn't want to mess up the spit curl she put in my hair for the photograph. Mom was known for spitting in her hand and then fixing our hair with it.

In her letter she wrote, "Here I am, gone forever, but I needed to leave you a letter to tell you I loved you so much. What a beautiful baby you were, all blonde, fair, and nicely packed. I spent more time with you than the other kids. I am so sorry you have had such a hard life. Please take care of yourself now."

She went on to say that she hated to leave us. But by the time I read her letter, she had found out what heaven is like and what God had prepared for her. She was so cute. She told me in the letter that if it were possible, she would blow gently into my face just to say hello. Mom ended her letter by saying how much she adored me and that I could and would overcome everything.

Disappointments are a fact of life and no one is immune to them. All of us have expectations of other people, ourselves, and yes, even God. There are two key reasons for disappointments: Firstly, we are disappointed by people, including ourselves, and secondly, we can be disappointed with our circumstances.

How we handle life's disappointments is extremely important. We must understand that this too shall pass, and tomorrow will come. Just don't give up; keep going! Circumstances are always changing, but there is one thing that never changes, and that is our God. Malachi 3:6 states, "For I am the Lord, I do not change." Jesus said in Hebrews 13:8, "He is the same yesterday, today and forever." I don't know why everyone doesn't get healed, but I do know this, it's not God's fault, and when things don't go the way we thought they should, we have to just trust Him and move on. If we don't, then we will allow the disappointments to destroy us—that is the entire purpose of disappointments.

I did a study on disappointment and the word "disappointment," according to Wikipedia.org, is "the feeling of dissatisfaction that follows the failure of expectations or hopes to manifest." If you break the word down, "dis" means to undo an action or indicates opposition. When the kids say don't "dis" me, that is what they are saying, whether they know that or not. They are saying, don't oppose me or undo me. The word "appoint" has a meaning of to fix or settle.

Interestingly enough, one definition of disappointment also means to remove from office, and that is what disappointment is trying to do. The devil will use that as an opportunity to steal your faith. Once he steals your faith, you are defeated—another "d" word. The whole purpose that the devil is trying to accomplish is to take us out of our rightful position in heaven. God's Word is already settled and fixed for us, but disappointment comes from the devil to undo what has already been fixed or settled in heaven. Disappointment is the seed of doubt that intrudes on our faith, and it is a strategy from the enemy to bring us down and then ultimately defeat us.

Losing my mom was the biggest disappointment I could face. I believed so hard for her, but it wasn't God's fault. He did heal her. It was the ultimate healing. She went to heaven. Death hurts, but my sister and mom are not lost. They may be dead in their bodies, but both of them are more alive than ever before. Death is not annihilation. It's separation. They both are separated from my family and me *temporally*. They have a new address, that's all.

The devil is so stupid. The biggest mistake he made was to give me that kind of disappointment right out of prison. Losing my mom three days out of prison after three years of believing in God topped the list of disappointments for me. Since coming home, I have had a lot of challenges and hurts, with great disappointments, but nothing has ever compared to losing my mom. So, the stupid jerk really has messed up with me, because if I didn't quit, then I am surely not going to quit now. There is a new day and this too shall pass, and it does.

I have regrets. Not being a daughter to my mom is one of them, not knowing Jesus from the beginning, not having a family with children. But "should've, could've, would've" doesn't get you anywhere. What is done is done. What I can do is make my mom proud and glorify God in all that I do now.

Regrets and disappointments are not the same. I had regrets from my past, and that is what regrets focus on, your past. Regrets focus on choices made in the past, which you cannot change. Disappointments focus on outcomes in the future. When we are disappointed, we set our sights on the future. That is exactly why we can't lose our faith and release the anchor of hope we have in Jesus and His Word. Our future is bright. The Word of God says so. Look at what Jeremiah 29:11 states in *The Message* Bible translation, "I know what I'm doing. I have it all planned out—plans to take care of you, not abandon you, plans to give you the future you hope for." Proverbs 13:12 in the NIV says, "Hope deferred makes the heart sick, but a longing fulfilled is a tree of life."

We will never go through life without being disappointed, but we don't have to let disappointments stop us. We get up, shake it off, and keep going. It takes determination and tenacity to not give up and keep pressing onto God. As Romans 8:28 makes clear, "We are assured and know that [God being a partner in their labor] all things work together and are [fitting into a plan] for good to and for those who love God and are called according to [His] design and purpose."

When I returned to the halfway house, I had no one. My mom had just died. My family was still upset with me. I had about thirty dollars to my name and no job. I was living behind a Goodwill store with seven women in the same room as me. I wasn't even able to mourn my mother when they told me she had died. I began to cry in my room when two of the girls who lived with me came in and said something so rude about my mom about her passing that it shut me down. There was no way I was going to let them see my emotions and expose myself to that abuse. Still through it all, He was there and I decided to use this disappointment as a stepping-stone and not a tombstone.

When I was in prison I dreamed of going to church. I would lie on my bunk and fantasize about what it was going to be like to be in a real church. I watched these beautiful African-American women going into church with their matching hats, dresses, shoes, and all the accessories. That is how I imagined myself going to church outside the prison walls. I couldn't wait to get to there and be baptized. I didn't want to get baptized behind bars, so I waited until my release. I wanted to be free both ways, free in the Spirit and free in the natural when I had my real baptism.

I had prayed and asked God for a dress to wear to church. In my three years in prison, I lost a lot of weight due to the fasting, walking, and the hard work outdoors. When I left my mom and dad's home, I took the clothes that my mom had packed for me. In the bag, there was a dress that fit me perfectly. In my old life, I was very boyish, so I didn't have a dress. But, here was a dress with shoes to match! To this day, I don't know where Mom got it or how she knew my size. It was God. I put that dress on and stood on a chair in front of the bathroom mirror and said out loud, "Here is your daughter, Mom, your little girl. Look at her now!" I wore that every Sunday for church. It was the dress I wore to my mother's funeral.

My Mom's body was flown to Indiana. That is where my entire family lives, except for my dad. My brother, aunt, and my mom's sister who helped care for her at the last, and my dad left for Indiana. Everyone at the halfway house said that I wouldn't be going to my mother's funeral, or if I did go it would be with a police escort and with handcuffs and shackles. I hadn't gone to my sister's funeral. I wasn't there for my family then and for me there was no way I was going to miss my mom's funeral, but I was prison property still. So, how was this going to happen? I went into my room after everyone else was gone to work and I prayed so hard for God to help me. There was no way I wanted to embarrass my family by appearing at Mom's funeral as a prisoner. I would not disgrace them like that anymore. I asked the Lord to please allow me to go without any escort and without any handcuffs and shackles. Everyone said I was crazy, it would never happen. I wouldn't listen.

That afternoon, I was called into the counselor's office and was released on a three-day furlough to go to my mother's funeral in Indiana. All the people at the halfway house dropped their jaws when they saw me with my bag in hand and all by myself. Without a guard or restraints, I climbed into the back of the taxicab that took me to the Tampa airport where I boarded a plane that flew me to Indiana. I was able to attend the funeral and be there for my family. My greatest prayer was, "God, please let me shine with You and let everyone see what You have done in me."

When I walked into the funeral home, people gasped. A cousin and her husband who had gotten saved and found Jesus during my incarceration jumped up and said, "You are saved, and you've got the Holy Ghost also!" Because of the Lord, I was able to fly to Indiana by myself, fly back without any restraints or embarrassment to the family, *and* without a prison official to watch me. That was the favor of God.

Chapter 14

This Isn't Jail House Religion

After returning from my mom's funeral, all I wanted to do is find a church to attend and find a job. I wanted to get to work, but my desire to find a church was even stronger.

There are many people who think people in jail or prison find what they call "jail house religion." Well, it's better than no religion at all. I shuddered to think what would have happened to me if ministries like Joyce Meyer's, Kenneth Copeland's, and others' were not there for prisoners like me. I thank God for those people who have not forgotten the prisoners. It isn't jailhouse religion, and it's not religion at all. Religion isn't going to help anyone in the first place. It's about having a relationship with the Lord. It's the Word of God and the planting of seeds into the hearts of men and women behind bars. How are they going to change if they don't hear the Word?

Jesus Himself proclaimed in John 6:63-65 from *The Message* translation, "The Spirit can make life. Sheer muscle and willpower don't make anything happen. Every word I've spoken to you is a Spirit-word, and so it is life-making." Just because some people who were in prison commit crimes again and return to prison doesn't mean we should stop trying to reach them. It took me seven arrests to get it, but the Word of Life finally stuck. My whole life has been transformed because of it.

If Jesus changed me and I was the worst of the worst, then He can change anyone. Don't assume because of their crimes that they don't deserve the gospel. The criminal is actually the best fit for the gospel. Jesus came for the sick, not the well, and not one of us deserves what Christ purchased for us on the cross with His death and resurrection. He died for all so that all could be forgiven. I am not saying we should excuse people's crimes or overlook them. There are always consequences for our bad choices. What I am saying is that love reaches out to the criminal and looks at the person to see what they can become with Christ as their Savior. Something happened in their life that makes them do what they are doing. Something became broken inside as it did with me. I thank God that He gave me another chance.

"Once a con always a con" is not true, just as "once an addict, always an addict" is a lie. If you believe that people remain an addict their entire lives, then you are accepting the world's belief over the truth of God's Word. This means His Word has no effect, and that limits the power of His Word in your life. The Bible says, "Who the Son sets free is free indeed" (John 8:36). Or, consider this one from 2 Corinthians 5:17: "If any man or women be in Christ He is a new creation or a new species all together, old things have passed away and all things have become new." Galatians 2:20 says, "It's no longer I who lives but Christ that lives in me and the life I use to live I live now by the faith of the Son of God." I get up on my soapbox about this because I hate to hear people say I am in recovery or I am an addict or alcoholic. If you know Jesus, then you aren't those things. You might be suffering with an addiction, but there is freedom in Christ. Who you are is a child of God, the righteousness of God, with a problem from which He can heal and deliver you. But, you must get in agreement with what He says about you, *not* what your circumstances say about you.

I tell you this with great love: We have to say what God says about us. If it's no longer I who lives, but it's Christ who lives in me. He is not an addict, nor an alcoholic. Just because you might have temptations and think about doing drugs or drinking or whatever, that doesn't mean that is who you are. Temptation will always be there, but God will also always give you a way out. If I were healed of cancer, would I keep saying that I am in recovery or recovering from cancer? Heavens, no! If I use to smoke and was delivered from that, do I tell people that I am a recovering smoker? Do I say, "Hi, my name is Teresa, and I am a smoker"? No again. I am free in Christ; I am a new creation, and I am the righteousness of God.

I had thirty dollars to my name. I took ten of that thirty and got quarters for the payphone that we used at the halfway house. I called local churches to see if they would come and give me a ride to church. One church after another refused to come, or they told me they didn't do that at their church. Finally, after several failed attempts, I found a church that agreed to come to get me and take me to church. It was an African-American church, and I was about the only white person in that place, but I didn't care. I had my new dress with matching shoes, and I just wanted to be in church. I loved being in a real church, even the pastor told me how much he was enjoying my presence. He said he hadn't seen someone enjoy church as much as me in a long time. If he only knew my life story!

I knew enough in my walk with the Lord to know that I desperately needed to be in fellowship with some other believers. I promised the Lord that day He touched me after my sister's death that I would serve

Him all the days of my life and I was going to keep that promise. I was amazed through all that time in the halfway house and after going home that I never wanted to go back to drugs or drinking. Life at the time was hard, but getting high wasn't an option anymore. I have struggles, but not with those things. I hate them with a passion. Why? Because I was delivered, I was free, indeed.

The counselor at the halfway house didn't want me to work so quickly after losing my mom, but I wanted to get far away from where I was staying. The worst thing for me was to sit around that place. I wanted to work. It's amazing the things that you take for granted throughout your life. For instance, the outdoors, fresh air, sunlight, the moon and stars, little animals, and God's creation.

How about privacy and personal boundaries? I didn't understand them until they were taken from me. Here's one most people don't think about: sitting with the light turned off, in complete darkness. Why would I do that? Because when you are in prison at no time are you in complete darkness. There is always a light throughout the dorm, so the guards can count you in the night. After three years of light always shining, it became tormenting. One of the first things I did when I arrived at the halfway house, when I was alone in my room, was turn the light switch off and sit in the dark. With great joy I would jump up and turn the light back on and then off again. I did that repeatedly, just because I could. I was so thankful for that, I was so thankful to be free and to have some choices now.

One of those choices was to get a job that would have fewer people and more outdoors. Being locked up with thousands of women over three years, I needed some space, plus I had a lot of processing to do and needed somewhere I could be with God. Since I had learned so much about mowing grass and horticulture while incarcerated, I started looking for a job in landscaping. I finally got an interview for a crew-member position at a landscaping company, and I wanted this job so badly. I prayed and asked God for it. I didn't know how hard it was going to be for me, but I wanted it.

Before I could get this job, I had to get my driver's license. That was another miracle in itself. While out there running from the law, I had tickets that hadn't been paid, and I only had twenty dollars to my name. So, I went to the driver's license branch and waited in line. The lady called my name and I went to the front. She checked my name in their records, as I was praying under my breath. I stood there for a moment, and then she said to look into the screen and read the letters on line three. After I finished, she said that it would be twenty dollars for my license.

I said, "Excuse me?"

She again stated, "Twenty dollars for your license. Pay me and then go over there to get your picture taken."

My picture had the biggest smile ever seen on a driver's license. Little did she know what a miracle God just worked? That landscaping job was mine!

On the way to the interview with the owner of the landscaping business, I got lost. I was an hour and a half late for the interview. I didn't know the Tampa bus system and got on the wrong bus. I had no money to call, so I walked around aimlessly trying to find where I was and where I was supposed to meet the owner. I had prayed for this job and I wanted it so badly. I finally went into a convenience store where I was able to get a quarter and call the owner.

As I was talking to him on the phone, I told him where I was and told him all the surroundings to identify my location. The owner told me to look across the four-lane highway in front of me and that he was located right across the street. I hung the phone up and ran as fast as I could across the highway. He was just about to leave, but, instead, he went ahead and gave me an interview. He told me that anyone who went through what I did trying to get a job deserved one. Because of the halfway house I was staying in, I was required to inform him that I was still federal property and what my charges were. He still gave me the job. I would start Monday morning!

Monday morning, I was at the owner's house bright and early ready to go. There he introduced me to his son and told me I would be on his crew. To work at this job, I had to have a pair of work boots, so I had to borrow some money from the halfway house to purchase a pair. The problem was I wasn't used to wearing shoes like that, and by mid-morning I had worn huge blisters on my feet. I had no money, and in fact, I had just used up all my bus passes except for the ride home. The owner's son, who was now my boss and I were working at a huge office building by the airport. We were picking up trash and getting ready to mow. The wind was blowing a cool breeze. The son was walking around, and all of the sudden he came cussing and yelling about something, so I went around the corner to see what was going on. As I turned the corner, I saw my boss's son snapping a ten and a five dollar bill in my face. He said, "Look what I found!"

You need to know up front something important about this guy. He was not a happy camper about my hiring. He was mad that his dad hired me, and he was going to do everything in his power to make me quit or scare me away. He was not a nice guy. On the first day, he said things like he was going to put a shotgun shell in my backpack so I would go back to prison. He also knew I loved the Lord, so he purposely got in my face and said God's name in vain. That was just on the first day!

When I saw the money that he found, I coveted that money. I said to myself, "That was my money, and I was supposed to find it, not him." Immediately, I asked the Lord to forgive me and I told the Lord that I trusted Him to help me, that I needed money to get bandages for my feet, and for the bus tickets to get to work. I said, "Lord, I know You will take care of me, and You will provide. Thank You for this job. I know You gave it to me, so You will work it out."

As God is my witness, I went to the other side of the parking lot, on this very windy day, and things were blowing all over the place. As I came around the corner, while picking up trash, I looked across the parking lot and saw something that seemed to be waving at me. I thought to myself, *What in the world is that?* so I walked closer, and the closer I got the more it waved, until I could tell that it was money.

I ran, just in case the wind would try to take it away. When I got to it, there sat a fifty-dollar bill! I grabbed that thing and started praising God right there in the parking lot. I went back to the owner's son and flashed my new find, my fifty dollars straight from heaven, and I said, as I snapped my fifty in his face, "Look what I found!"

He didn't say much the rest of the day. With that fifty dollars God had given me, I first put five back for my tithe, got two weeks of bus passes, bandages for my feet, and paid for my work boots.

I hurt from the first day of work. When I got off the bus, the men at the halfway house began to make bets that I wouldn't make it on this job. They gave me two weeks before I would quit. I felt like God gave me this job, no matter how hard it became. It was tough, but I wasn't going to let go of it.

The second day of work was pure hell. The boss's son pulled out all the stops. He was having me pull huge trees out of a vacant lot and doing things that he didn't require the other man on the team to do. This guy didn't like me and again he threatened me about doing something to send me back to prison. When I got off the bus, the guys at the center were laughing and predicted it wouldn't be long before it was over for me. I limped along the road and up the stairs to go inside. I went to take a hot shower. My hands were bleeding, my feet were bleeding, and I was dirty. I looked like a raccoon from the dirt on my face and the white part where my sunglasses covered my eyes. When I got in the shower, the water hitting my hands and feet felt like sharp knives going through them. I started to cry with the pain. I was determined; I couldn't quit. I don't know why I was doing that to myself. I think I just wanted to prove that I could do this, and I couldn't think about working a job inside or around a lot of people right then.

While in the shower, I started praying to God and asking Him to help me. I remembered the testimony of Brother Hagin when the Lord had healed him when he was bedridden with an incurable heart disease. The Lord healed him, but he wasn't used to manual labor. He hadn't built his muscles up for that kind of work. He prayed and asked the Lord to help him do the physical labor and the Lord did. Brother Hagin said in his book that he out worked all the men in the lumber-yard. He worked more than ten men put together.

So, I told the Lord, "Well, I know You don't play favorites, so if You did that for him, then You will do it for me. Please help me to have the strength throughout the day to work, Lord, no matter what task he puts me through."

The next day when I went to work, I worked as hard as the guy on the crew, and I was even stronger than I had ever been. I was amazed at how I was feeling and what I was doing. When I got off the bus the guys weren't laughing as much. I was limping and in pain the first couple of days of work, but then I was skipping right along and walking upright. Within two weeks it was like nothing for me, and the men at the center and the boss's son knew I wasn't going to give up.

After two weeks though, I couldn't take the boss's son anymore. It wasn't the work. It was his attitude toward me. He was so mean! At the end of the day, I went to talk with the owner and thank him for giving me a chance, and tell him I wouldn't be able to work for him anymore. I didn't say anything about his son, but when I told him that I would have to look for another job, he told me, "That's too bad you are leaving. I need a crew leader for my other crew, someone I can trust, and I was thinking about you." Now, mind you, I had just been released from prison, and this man said he trusted me! I looked at him in amazement. I hadn't heard that in a long time. Before I could say anything, he asked me if I was quitting because of his son and I told him yes. He said, "He is a real jerk, isn't he?" I said, "I wouldn't say that," and the owner said, "I would, he is a jerk!" So, the owner told me if I would stay on he would make me a crew leader with my own equipment and a company truck to drive. And, I wouldn't be with his son anymore. I agreed and took the job.

The company truck wasn't just for work. I was able to drive it back to the halfway house and the owner actually put gas in it and let me drive it home to see my dad, who was an hour away from me. This was such the favor of the Lord. I had just gotten out of prison, and I had been in prison for credit card fraud and theft, yet this man was giving me all his lawn equipment to be responsible for—his company truck and a gold MasterCard (his personal credit card) that I used to put gas in the truck and the equipment. Not only was *that* amazing, but I got to drive all over Tampa, down by the beach and all over the area, working on yards and plants.

The only problem about my new position was something the owner didn't tell me—I was the only crew-member. This was not a problem. God had answered my prayer! I had a job all to Jesus and me. I was working outdoors with my own transportation, all this after just a little over two weeks out of prison!

The next time I returned to the halfway house, it didn't require me getting off the bus. Instead, I was driving the company truck. Also, my limp when walking up to the house was gone.

All those people who were laughing and making bets on me were not laughing anymore. They actually started to respect me. I would leave for work in the morning, driving the truck. Some of the men who had bet on me quitting would be waiting at the bus bench. I would honk my horn and wave as I drove by. I couldn't help myself! I worked that job for six months until I went back to my hometown. I would ride on the lawnmower with my headset on, listening to Christian music, singing at the top of my lungs to the Lord. While it was hard work, it was also what I needed.

Chapter 15

Transformation and Restoration

If I were going to quit at any point of my journey, it would have been upon my release from the halfway house. I didn't mourn my mom and that is why I actually was dreading going back home where I'd be surrounded with memories of her.

I saw my dad a few times after my mom's death, but that was it. Coming home to an empty house filled with the scents of my mother, her clothes, and all her belongings was quite difficult. Also, over the years my relationship with my dad had deteriorated, so this move was not the best scenario for me. I had no other place to go. I had to face it head-on and it wasn't easy.

The entire time I was in prison, as I have said throughout this entire book, the two ministries that helped me the most were Kenneth Copeland's and Joyce Meyer's. They never stopped sending me magazines, books, and anything else that would help me in my walk with the Lord. You have no idea what an impact their materials made on me unless you experienced a significant amount of time living behind prison walls.

These particular ministries care so much, and they demonstrate how much they really do care by sending materials knowing I had no way to pay for them. They gave me things for free, just to help me. I use their names a lot to honor the men and women of God who helped me. I am so grateful for men and women who do prison ministry and I am so thankful for all the volunteers who ministered to me while I was incarcerated. How could I have changed if I didn't hear the Word of God taught and preached? When we read the gospels, we find that Jesus always went to where the criminals, prostitutes, winebibbers, and the outcasts were. He loved the outcasts and the throwaways, and He is no different today. When the world says someone is useless and no good, the Lord says they are perfect and wonderfully made as His workmanship. I love that about Him so much. He never says someone is not worth it. On the contrary, He extends His arms of love to everyone who will receive Him.

If I were going to quit, it would have been the day I arrived home. I came home to the smell of my mom and an estranged relationship with my dad. In fact, in the last letter that mom left me before she died, she had begged me to please be my dad's friend and to build a relationship with him. That wasn't going to happen overnight. In fact, it would take years.

Also, I had to pack up my mom's belongings that were still in the house and get rid of them. It was an extremely lonely time, and it was very hurtful.

The emotions that I pushed aside for all those months, and even years, came on me full force—anger, resentment, unforgiveness, and lack of self-worth. These were directed mainly toward myself, but also toward others, like my dad. Everything within me said to just quit, give up, but God had a plan to propel me forward. He had already prepared a miracle for me to help push me through and not quit.

I was released in February 2000. That is what the prison records showed, but I didn't get home until the end of June/beginning of July of 2000 because of the six months I had to do in the halfway house.

Dad picked me up in Tampa. Arriving home I walked on the porch, and sitting on the table was a package addressed to me from Joyce Meyer Ministries. I asked Dad what it was and he said he thought that I had ordered something, but I hadn't. I quickly opened the package and inside was a letter from her ministry congratulating me on my release. Now mind you, I was released in February, but the package came two weeks before I got home in July. The letter said they were happy I was home and that they hoped this would help me in my walk with the Lord.

Inside the package was a tape series called "I Am Determined." You don't know what a turning point that was for me, because I knew it was directly from God. It was a word from God in due course, at just the right time, to propel me toward God, to provide the determination I needed. I put my headset on and listened to her teaching over and over again. In this teaching the Lord kept saying to me, "Don't give up. I have a good plan for your life. Just don't give up. Have a holy determination not to give up, just keep going."

Throughout this whole series the Lord encouraged me, and I would hear all the scriptures He had already given me before my release. The Lord would say, "I will give you a hope and a future and for your former shame I will recompense you double. What the enemy meant for harm I will turn it to your good."

The most important thing about this part of my story is that I didn't give up, and still haven't seventeen years later. Given up to what, you ask? There is nothing from this world that I want. I had the things of this world. I had all the partying, all the things the flesh wanted. If my flesh screamed for something, it got it, but what did it produce? It produces nothing but death, destruction, and complete destitution.

Galatians 5:17 states, "For the desires of the flesh are opposed to the [Holy] Spirit and the [desires of the] Spirit are opposed to the flesh (godless human nature); for these are antagonistic to each other [continually withstanding and in conflict with each other], so that you are not free but are prevented from doing what you desire to do." I have lived both sides: the losing side and the winning side. I would take the winning side with Jesus any day. My worst days with the Lord are so much better than my best days with the devil, or what I thought were "best" days.

The Lord put something in my heart about willpower. So many people think that it's your willpower that will help you, but that is opposite to what God says. As long as I used my willpower over me, I got into all kinds of trouble. When I learned to submit my will to God, I found God-power. Thanks to that God-power, I don't get into the messes I did before. The last thing you need is willpower; we need God-power, the power of the Holy Spirit and the resurrection power of the Lord Jesus Christ.

Galatians 5:16 makes it clear: "But I say, walk and live [habitually] in the Holy Spirit [responsive to and controlled and guided by the Spirit]; then you will certainly not gratify the cravings and desires of the flesh (of human nature without God)." Notice how God said, "habitually." This is a daily process and sometimes a minute-by-minute process. Not my will but your will be done God.

The Message Bible states in Romans 8:11-17,

> It stands to reason, doesn't it; that if the alive-and-present God who raised Jesus from the dead moves into your life, He'll do the same thing in you that He did in Jesus, bringing you alive to Himself? When God lives and breathes in you (and he does, as surely as He did in Jesus), you are delivered from that dead life. With

His Spirit living in you, your body will be as alive as Christ's! So don't you see that we don't owe this old do-it-yourself life one red cent? There's nothing in it for us, nothing at all. The best thing to do is give it a decent burial and get on with your new life. God's Spirit beckons. There are things to do and places to go! This resurrection life you received from God is not a timid, grave-tending life. It's adventurously expectant, greeting God with a childlike "What's next, Papa?" God's Spirit touches our spirits and confirms who we really are. We know who He is, and we know who we are: Father and children.

I didn't give into the pressure. I was tempted once to go back to using drugs and alcohol, but it was just a temptation, and the Lord provided a way out for me. Since that day, when I was released over thirteen years ago, thanks to the Lord, I have never been tempted to go back to how I used to be or want to take drugs. I am free and I am so thankful! It has been over seventeen years since the Lord first set me free that July morning in 1997.

Have I had challenges in my life? Yes, of course, but not with drugs because they are dead in my life. Drugs and alcohol are severed from my very being, never to return

After getting situated with my dad, I felt the Lord wanted me to start college. I enrolled in a community college in my hometown where for the first two years I was Phi Theta Kappa and had a 4.0 grade-point average. This proves that God can heal you, and He can transform you. I graduated and would have preferred putting Jesus's name on the diploma because He did every bit of it.

About six years from my release, I went back to school and obtained my bachelor of science degree in psychology from Florida Southern College. I think it is funny that the Lord would have me study about the human mind when I was told that I wouldn't have any mind left. He is in the restoration business—nothing missing and nothing broken.

Going back to get my degree was another miracle from the Lord. I had no interest in going back to finish school, but the Lord wanted it. I already had some student loans and didn't want to go further into debt, so I told the Lord that if He wanted me to go back to school, then He would have to pay for it.

I was at my desk in my office at work and the phone rang. It was a lady who helped support the ministry I worked for. She questioned why I wasn't attending school, and I told her that I didn't want the loans over my head. Her next statement made me cringe, "I will pay for your school, just finish your degree!" That was over $20,000 that this lady gave me as a "scholarship!"

When I was in prison, I would dream of meeting Joyce Meyer face-to-face to say thank you, especially after I got that package from her ministry. In October 2000, she was coming to a church in Tampa and, believe me, I was the first person in line waiting for the doors to open. I prayed that God would let me get so close that I could see her arched eyebrows. He did. I was in the second row for almost all the meetings. As I walked to the bathroom, I saw a lady selling cassette tapes at a book table. It was Joyce's daughter! As I walked past I felt the Lord tell me to go and tell her thank you, but I walked by. I was too scared to do that. Finally, I felt Him continuing to tug at me to go over to Joyce's daughter. So, on the way back to my seat, I stopped and told the story of how much their ministry helped me while I was in prison and how much I appreciated receiving that package upon arriving home. I told

Joyce's daughter that she was the closest I could get to her mom to say how much I was thankful for all that her ministry did for me. And then Joyce's daughter said me, "Why don't you to tell her yourself?"

When I got back to my seat and Joyce came out on the stage, she called me up to share my testimony about how the Lord had set me free from eighteen years of addiction and that I had just been released from prison. She had helped me so much! The Lord used her in a mighty way. The thousand people in attendance went wild cheering for me, and I got to hug her and tell her thank you personally. God is so good! You will see later why that is an important part of my story and needs to be shared.

That day was the beginning of more blessings and restoration that God was planning in my walk with Him. It meant so much for me for the Lord to do that. The entire time I was in prison I would say, "One day I will be able to thank her in person for all their kindness toward me." The Lord arranged that for me. Through it all, the Lord kept confirming to me, "Hey Teresa, I am here. I've got you, you are mine, and I am not letting go. Just don't let go of me."

God is in the restoration and transformation business. Restoration means renewal, revival, or reestablishment. I like the last one: reestablishment. God reestablishes us to our rightful position with Him in Christ. Restoration also means to return something to a former, original, normal, or unimpaired condition. God restores His masterpiece to its original state and intent.

In my imagination, I picture God creating the world like a great painter with a blank canvas. On the first day, He began to paint the stars and sky and the heavens with all the light. Then, He painted the waters and the Earth with all its plants, flowers, and beauty. Then, God decided to paint all the awesome animals He has given us richly to enjoy. And, as any great artist does, He stepped back and looked at what He painted. He said what He had just done was good, but something was missing! As He rubbed His chin and examined the painting even further, He said, "I know what is missing!" and He took His paintbrush and begins to finish His masterpiece by painting you, everyone, and me across the globe, as the sands are on the seashore. He continued to paint people. Then, He said, "Now, it's perfect! My masterpiece is complete because I have made them in My image and in My likeness."

A masterpiece made by the Painter's hand, that's us. In our lives, as we walk away from His original intent for our lives, we become like a valuable painting that no one realized was valuable, hidden away in an attic oblivious to the fact that the painting was priceless.

One day, a man comes by, His name is Jesus. He is an Inspector of fine art, and He sees the valuable masterpiece, torn, dusty, and unwanted. He says, "Can I buy this from you? I will trade My life for this masterpiece that you have just thrown away," and with this purchase, the Art Inspector takes it with Him to His palace, cleans it up, and restores the painting to its original state and then He puts it on display for all to see and enjoy. After seeing this display of art and how it has been restored, people of all ages, colors, and nationalities from all over begin to go through their attics to see what painting He could restore for them, so that gallery after gallery of masterpieces are on display for the whole world to see.

To restore means to bring back its former state, to bring back from a state of ruin, decay, disease, and to bring back to its owner, to make good or to make amends. Immediately after giving my life to the Lord, He began restoring things back to my life. For my former shame, He gives you twice the honor. The restoration process doesn't happen overnight. After all, for thirty-six years of my life, I basically served the world, the flesh, and the devil, and out of those thirty-six years, half those years were a blur due to drug addiction.

So, what is my point here? Well, some of the restoration from God came quickly, but most has taken time. He wants to work things out of me so He can get things *in* me and *to* me. Jeremiah 30:17 states, "For I will restore health to you, and I will heal your wounds, says the Lord, because they have called you an outcast, saying, this is Zion, whom no one seeks after and for whom no one cares!"

The Lord spoke to my heart after returning home and shared Joel 2:25, "And I will restore or replace for you the years that the locust has eaten-the hopping locust, the stripping locust, and the crawling locust." And, my favorite verse is found in Zechariah 9:12 in the same version: "Return to the stronghold [of security and prosperity], you prisoners of hope; even today do I declare that I will restore double your former prosperity to you." I have and continue to see how the Lord is restoring to me everything that has been stolen, even from my own bad choices. He still has had mercy on me.

Just this year, after being thirteen years released from prison, I went to Orlando to hear Joyce Meyer preach. She was in the downtown area and I had stayed for the weekend. The second day of her conference, I decided to walk to the venue that morning and enjoy the gorgeous day that the Lord had given us.

As I stepped out of the hotel lobby, there was a limousine sitting out front, so I did what most of us do. I got nosy to see who was in the back seat. As I bent down the driver looked at me and asked me if I was going to the conference, and I told him yes I was. Then he said, "Let me give you a ride." Well, at first I said no. I simply wanted to walk and he continued to tell me that he would be honored to take me, so I agreed. I have never ridden in a limousine before. So, I had to keep telling myself not to open the door, let the driver do that for you. As I got in the back, I knew it was the Lord honoring me. He took me to the venue and, I must say, all eyes were on me to see if I was perhaps famous—a far cry to what I used to be!

Why am I sharing this story? To show you how God restored me. He gave me honor to replace my former shame. When I left the conference that afternoon, I walked back to the hotel. I noticed a tall building that was being guarded. It was the Federal Courthouse Building. Thirteen years ago, I rode in the back of a SUV in shackles and handcuffs to that very building. It was where I was sentenced to federal prison. This time, instead of being in shackles and handcuffs, I was completely free. I had ridden in the back of a limousine right past that federal building. This time, I was being treated like a queen or royalty.

While attending the community college, I felt the Lord prompting me into ministry. That was my heart's desire. I love to tell people about what the Lord has done in my life. I felt He wanted me to walk away from college to enter into full-time ministry, and that is what I did.

Eventually I did go back and finish my education. It's important to finish what you start, so I went back later while still working in ministry.

The lady I spoke about who ministered to me in the jail after I first got saved, her husband wanted to open a transitional house for women coming out of prison. It housed up to ten women, and, to be honest, that wasn't where I wanted to be. I truly wanted to go off to Bible school—real Bible school—but God had different plans. I was going to learn while in the trenches, on-the-job training and the school of hard knocks. I was hired as a house mom and eventually started working full-time as a coordinator to another ministry that helped women coming out of prison. They also had a transitional home where the women would come and be trained in the Word as well as in life skills. I was with this ministry for over nine years, until 2010. I just couldn't take anymore. I wanted to share with the world what Jesus has done, especially in Africa.

About three years after my release, I applied to return to the prisons to preach. Thanks to the Lord, for over ten years now I have been doing prison ministry—here in Florida and in other nations. It's such an honor from God to be able to share hope with men and women who would otherwise have no hope at all. Isn't this what Christianity is all about, sharing what was freely given to you, giving it away to others?

The Lord placed me in jail ministry in the same jail where I had been incarcerated. The Lord actually arranged a meeting with a candidate for Sheriff of our county who asked me the secret to my success. I told him it was Jesus, of course! I also said that if I had been arrested in his county, I wouldn't have made it because there was hardly any church in that jail. I continued to explain that I was placed in a faith-based dorm that helped me to grow and get established in righteousness.

I told the soon-to-be Sheriff that what he needed in this county was a faith-based program for men and women. That was about eight or nine years ago, and now the jail I was incarcerated in has church continuously. After his election, he began a faith-based program where I teach every Friday night. How awesome is that? God is amazing!

I had moved away from my dad's house for a few years, but that didn't mean the problem with our relationship went away. Avoidance isn't freedom and it isn't victory. To get free, you have to face the things of your past head on. The secrets you keep inside are the ones that will keep you sick. You have to look back and carefully examine things in your past to allow the Lord to heal those areas, but don't stay there.

I like this statement I read on *Facebook*, "You can't look backwards and forwards at the same time. Where you came from doesn't determine where you are going!" Our past doesn't have to dictate our future. It can propel us into a great destiny with God if we allow Him to use our past for His Glory. There is a healing process we must go through in order to move forward. In the book of Numbers, in the Bible, the Israelites remained in their past being slaves. When they were about to enter the Promised Land, most of the people saw themselves as grasshoppers, and only two saw themselves in the truth of God's Word. They were healed from their pasts and moved on while the others remained in that grasshopper mentality.

If I don't see that something is in need of restoration, there will be no restoration. It's like looking at a piece of broken furniture in need of repair, but you see it as showroom-ready. If that's that case, there will never be any restoration. I had to look at things through God's eyes to see that I had a lot of broken-down furniture that needed to be repaired, but only He could do it.

Before I came to Jesus, I was a shack with broken furniture inside, worn and torn, pulled out of someone's dumpster or the city dump. But when I gave Jesus entrance to my heart, He moved in and the shack turned into a mansion. The old furniture had to be moved out to make room of the fine expensive furniture that God provides us through His Spirit. So, the furniture that was worn, like pride, self-hatred, unforgiveness, lust, greed, and all that goes with the fallen nature, had to be thrown out. He had to make room for love, joy, peace, helping others, loving God, and doing good instead of evil. This fine furniture from heaven could now be moved in. This process is not an overnight one. Some things come quickly, but other things take time and determination. God does it for us, but He needs a willing vessel that will commit to never give up and keep pressing on until the moving process is over.

This brings me to the concept of transformation. To be transformed means to be changed in form, appearance, nature, or character. The *Webster's Revised Unabridged Dictionary* states that the word means to change the form of, to change or metamorphose as a caterpillar is transformed into a butterfly. The Bible states in Romans 12:1, "I appeal to you therefore, brethren, and beg of you in view of [all] the mercies of God, to make a decisive dedication of your bodies [presenting all your members and faculties] as a living sacrifice, holy (devoted, consecrated) and well pleasing to God, which is your reasonable (rational, intelligent) service and spiritual worship." Verse 2 goes on to say, "Do not be conformed to this world (this age), [fashioned after and adapted to its external, superficial customs], but be transformed (changed) by the [entire] renewal of your mind [by its new ideals and its new attitude], so that you may prove [for yourselves] what is the good and acceptable and perfect will of God, even the thing which is good and acceptable and perfect [in His sight for you]."

The more I study the Word of God, the more the Word has gradually transformed me. The more I allow the Word to transform my ways of doing, being, and thinking, the more restoration can come into my life.

I learned how the Word works and restores, especially after moving back into my dad's house. For years, I had this rage toward him. It wasn't my dad's fault, even though I kept blaming him. I had unhealthy expectations of my dad that he was not able to meet. I had a void in my heart and needed more from my dad, but he wasn't able to fill that void.

Only God could be the Father that I craved. Only He could fill that void. People can't meet our needs, only God can. I wanted my dad to be a certain way, talk a certain way, and love me a certain way. I was wrong to look to my dad as a source of comfort and to expect him to change. *I* was the one who needed to change. God has to become our source for everything.

Oh, how I prayed! I knew I was supposed to love my dad and honor him, but I didn't know how to do that. First, he was an authority figure in my life. I didn't realize that I had an issue with authority, especially men in authority. So, that had to change.

It didn't happen overnight, it was a long process with me. It would have probably gone more quickly if I wasn't so full of pride and if I had worked with God rather than against Him. That is why it's so important that no matter how painful it is, you have to see yourself in the Light of God's Word. We will have imperfections along our journey in life, but imperfections are not the same as impurities. Those impure things must be brought to the cross and severed from our life. That is what Christianity is all about: God's image and being like God.

For me, God had to deal with bitterness, the root of rejection, and unforgiveness one-by-one; God had to starting cutting the roots away. The forgiveness issue was hard, but one of the things that helped me the most was finding out that forgiving someone is a choice. If I choose to forgive and make that choice to honor God, then He handles the rest of all the emotions that go with it. I know from experience that He does come through for you.

I felt the Lord move me closer to my dad, and this is where the rubber hit the road. After years of fighting with God, and myself, I finally surrendered. I chose to do it God's way. You know love never fails.

The first thing He started having me to do was serve my dad. So, I started making him dinner. Next, I had to stop being bossy around the house and not to expect so much from him. God is my source of everything, if I look to people for love and acceptance, I will always be disappointed. I have disappointed people, so what makes me think other people should walk perfectly before me? I had to release people and let them be imperfect but let them be who God made them to be. I wanted to be released to be who God created me to be. I also had to learn to look at my dad with the eyes of the Lord, not with the judgment that was in my heart. When I started to look to God for my source of comfort and love, and, yes, as my Father, then things started to change. It wasn't my dad that had changed, I had changed. My dad is so sweet and kind, but through all that junk that was in my heart, I couldn't see it.

This past year has been the best time in my life with my dad. God has restored me a father and daughter relationship that I desired so badly. He is who he is and I am who I am, and we love each other. I had the great privilege of leading my dad to the Lord. We went to church together, too. As I sat in the back row with my dad in his church—he calls it the old quiet church—I wrapped my arms around him, with tears streaming down my face. I heard the Lord say to me, "I am giving you no regrets!" That is true restoration right there!

My dad will be eighty-six years old this year, and I know when he goes on to be with the Lord, I will have peace in our house, peace with my lovely dad and no regrets similar to what I had with my sister and my mom. Just think, if I hadn't done it God's way, I would still be fighting and miserable, but now I am so happy! I "died" to my will and let God's power take over. Now, I have a daddy on earth, and one in Heaven. You can't go wrong with that!

More transformation had to take place in my life concerning my true identity. I was involved in a lot of sexual perversion when I was without the Lord. It took a long time to renew my mind and submit areas of my heart that had been scarred from abuse and exposure to things contrary to the ways of God.

When I came to the Lord, I made up my mind that there was no going back and that I would serve Him no matter the cost. I didn't want to be the way I was, but there was nothing I could do about it. The Lord had to do it for me. So, the more I tried, the more frustrated I became. I would attempt to change the outside, like how I dressed, the hair, the make-up, but that didn't work because it was my heart that had to change. When the insides get changed, then the outside automatically changes. You don't have to force it because it has been done for you naturally.

I needed deliverance and a willingness to keep saying, "Lord, I love you more, and I want to be the way you have made me, your original plan—not my feelings and ideas based on deception and lies."

Think about how full of pride it is to look at God and say to Him that He didn't make us right. Such pride! Such arrogance!

I would have images of the abuse and what I had exposed myself to. Sitting in church, these things would come across my mind and I would feel so ashamed. I could be talking with people and things would come up from my heart that I didn't want to be there. I prayed and fasted, and prayed and fasted again. I had people pray for me and I still had the issues. The images came to steal and kill my identity in Christ. The enemy used my past to try to convince me that I was the same and something was wrong with me. I had to submit those impurities in my heart and in my thinking to God. He took care of them, but it didn't happen overnight. Now, I am rendered whole in this way. He has set me free and given me a wonderful security in myself. I know who I am in Him, and I love that.

For years, I fought with the issue of my sexual identity. I loved God, and I still love God with all my heart. I finally decided to tell people what I was going through. No matter what they thought, I had to get it out in the open. I felt that if I kept it hidden and didn't expose what was happening inside me and the torment that was in my mind, then I liked it and I was in agreement with those feelings. So, I started telling some of my friends every time an attack would come. Eventually, I noticed, after much prayer, reading the Word, and fasting, that the attacks weren't coming from my inside anymore. I don't know when God did it, but He delivered me, and then I noticed that the attacks were coming from the outside, trying to get back in. That is when I knew I had victory, thanks to God.

We overcome by the blood of the Lamb and the word of our testimony. But the devil comes back to see if your house is clean and in order. So he would come and stare at me to see if my house was in order and, thanks to the Lord, it was. Through confession, confessing God's Word, and surrendering all to Him, I was able to overcome.

I now have a whole new attitude about men, marriage, and about myself. I love being a woman of God. I love being a lady. I am beautiful inside and out. Years ago I would never have been able to say that. Am I married? Not yet. The Lord hasn't brought anyone yet, but I don't have to be married to prove I am free. The Bible says in Matthew 5:16, "Let your good deeds before men glorify your Father." Perhaps there will be another book about how the Lord brought me a husband!

Some things were stolen from me that I've had to accept. For example, I will never know what it is like to be a mother and have my own child. I will never have a family album with photos of my children. I am too old to have kids now.

I will will not be able to spend time with my mother until I get to heaven, and I can't bring my sister back.

I used to ask the Lord, "How do you restore my mom and sister and how will you restore not having a family and home like most people?"

God has restored my mom, my sister and me by giving me spiritual moms and sisters all over the world. In fact, I have so many sisters and moms that I can't keep up with them.

Jesus raised the babies I aborted in heaven. They are there with my mother and sister. When I get to heaven, I will be in my mansion with my children. I know this will happen because with God all things are possible. I can have a large wall in my mansion with my kids' pictures on it. I also get all of eternity to be with my mom and sister.

The Lord encouraged me before leaving on a mission trip about not having any children. Since then my heart is at peace. He shared Isaiah 54:1, "Sing, O barren one, you who did not bear; break forth into singing and cry aloud, you who did not travail with child! For the [spiritual] children of the desolate one will be more than the children of the married wife, says the Lord." Everywhere I go now people call me "Mama."

When I left my job of nine years, I took a huge step of faith. I went from having a salary to not having a salary at all, but it was worth it for me to go out into the world preaching the Gospel.

Before leaving my job, I had attended a Joyce Meyer women's conference in St. Louis with a friend. I noticed the *Hand of Hope* booth for their medical mission's outreach. It explained that volunteers could go on mission trips. I filled out an application and submitted it. Several months later, I received an e-mail from them.

The e-mail from Joyce Meyer Ministries said, "Congratulations, you have been accepted as a volunteer on our medical mission team" and it included a schedule of upcoming trips. The first place they were going was Zimbabwe. I knew I had to go! I have one chance in this life, and the first half wasn't so great, but after all the Lord has done for me, I wasn't going to sit by and do nothing more for Him. I went for it! I left my job in 2010. As I walked away from my job of nine years, I heard in my spirit the words, "Run, Teresa, Run!"

Since then I have traveled to Africa more than ten times and once to India. Who would have thought that God would let me have the great privilege of going to the nations and preaching the gospel of Jesus Christ? And, to top it off, it is through a ministry that helped me so much while I was incarcerated. That is, again, the restoration of the Lord.

This trip was my first trip ever to Africa and it was amazing! The Lord took me from crack houses to villages in Africa to see Him work. I was doing prison ministry and jail ministry, but I had never shared the gospel in another country. I was scared. But, I know that it isn't about me, it's about Him working *through* me.

It might not seem like I am the best candidate to be used by the Lord. I was a drug addict and an ex-con, but that is what is so wonderful about God. He makes you brand new, just like He did with Paul in the Book of Acts. Paul committed genocide in the name of God before he was dramatically transformed. Paul thought he was doing right by killing Christians, but God changed him and used him for good. God will use anyone who will make himself or herself available to Him.

I saw so many miracles on these mission trips. Oh, I had fun, but I really didn't know what I was doing. I simply said what the Word says and the Word and Jesus did the rest. A young boy's grandmother brought him to the place where we were preaching the gospel. This boy couldn't talk. He was mute. His grandmother brought him to the ministry building believing that God would heal him. After I prayed for him, the Lord opened his mouth, and the first word that came forth from him was Jesus. I told him to say it again. He continued to repeat Jesus's name as they walked away,

Jesus is still a Healer. I am proof of that, and so are so many other people who the Lord touched on these trips. I still have a cane that a very tall man in Zimbabwe had when he walked into the ministry where we were preaching.

As I looked at him, I asked if He believed the Lord could heal him. After I preached the Word and this man received Christ as his Savior, I walked over and laid hands on him to pray for healing. I first touched his knees, and he stood up and started marching all over the room without his cane! Then, he asked me to pray for his back. As I prayed for his back, I told him to do what he couldn't do before. All of the sudden this man bent over and touched his toes! He went up and down. I couldn't stop him if I tried! He began bending over again and then started marching around the room. It was awesome! He gave me his cane, and I brought it home with me. I still have it to remind me of how awesome our God is.

A lady in India was riddled with arthritis and pain. She was in a wheelchair; she couldn't walk. In fact, when I lightly laid my hands on her, she screamed in pain. I remember that as they wheeled her away, I saw no healing for her and my heart was broken. I hate to see someone in pain like that. As I walked away, I felt so bad.

The Lord spoke to my heart and said, "Just because you didn't see her get healed doesn't mean she didn't get healed."

The next day as I was beginning to preach, one of the interpreters ran over and interrupted me and said, "Mama Teresa, please come, you have to come now!"

Running across the courtyard, I followed him as he led me into a dormitory where the elderly were housed. As I turned the corner, there was the lady who was riddled with pain the day before, but now she was showered and sitting with her legs up on the bed—completely healed. When she saw me she started to cry and called for me to come over. She kissed my hands and then started kissing my forehead and my cheeks. We rejoiced together about how the Lord healed her. There is nothing more priceless than that—except Jesus of course—but that is Him. He is mighty to save and heal!

The Lord gave me a scripture found in Isaiah 54:1 about my spiritual children. I was given this Scripture before my trip to India, and also before my trip to Ethiopia in 2010. Ever since I received this verse from the Lord, everywhere I go, into the jails, the prisons, the nations, people call me Mama Teresa. Do you know how the Lord has restored a family to me? By giving me spiritual children all over the world. I can't tell you how many souls have come into the Kingdom of God because of the testimony the Lord has given me.

Every time the Lord allows me to bring someone to Him, God gives me another child to put on the wall in my hallway. My child, my spiritual children, didn't cause me the pain of natural childbirth, and I didn't get stretch marks either! Thanks to the Lord, I have kids in Florida, Indiana, Madagascar, Zimbabwe, India, South Africa, Ethiopia, and the Philippians, and I am just getting started!

So many wonderful things have happened. Have there been hard times? Yes, of course. Have there been challenges? Yes, of course. But through it all, He has been with me. I am forever changed. I am a masterpiece made by the Master's hands.

If you don't know Jesus, can I simply tell you that you are missing out? Nothing is worth more than having Him. My purpose is to tell people what He has done for me. Secondly, I need more kids to put on my wall! More importantly, I can't help but share someone as wonderful as Jesus. He is real and He loves you.

The Bible states in John 3:16, "That God so loved the world that He gave His only begotten Son, that whoever believes in Him shall not perish but have everlasting life." Jesus gave us everything He is. In exchange, He asks for you to give Him all you are. What a trade! He gives you His beauty for your ashes.

Let me help you come to Him. If you are serious, want a new life, and are finished, tired of doing the same things over and over again and getting nowhere, say this prayer with me. Mean it from the bottom of your heart. Say it out loud as you read it: "Lord I ask you to forgive me of all my sins. Your Word says that if I confess with my mouth and believe in my heart that Jesus is the Son of God, I shall be saved. Jesus, I confess that you are the Son of God, come into my heart. Today I make you the Lord of my life. I turn my back on the world, and today I make you my Lord and Savior. Amen."

You are now a new creation in Christ. It's important that you gather with strong Christians, get a Bible, and start learning about the Lord. Remember, it is a process, so don't beat yourself up when you make mistakes. You will. So, don't run from God, run *to* Him. He won't push you away. He will love you until you can love yourself.

Find a good on-fire-for-God church and surround yourself with winners. When you hang around winners, you become a winner. Just know that I love you, and I am grateful to the Lord that He allowed me to share what He has done in me and through me. Feel free to connect with me. My contact information is at the back of the book.

One more thing before closing...

When I was in jail, I received the baptism of the Holy Spirit. You must have the power of God to make it. Study about the baptism of the Holy Spirit. I am not about denominations. We belong to Jesus, and that's it. I am about the truth of God's Word, and the baptism of the Holy Spirit is for whomever wants it. You just gave yourself to the Lord, or maybe you have been a Christian for a while but have never asked for the power of God. Please get wisdom and understanding.

I want to lead you in another prayer, and it's to receive the baptism of the Holy Spirit with the evidence of speaking in tongues.

Say this prayer with me:

> As a child of God, Father, You said in Your Word that if I ask anything according to Your Word that You will give it to me, anything according to your will. Father I know that it is Your will for me to have power from on high. When I received Jesus as my Lord and my Savior, I received the Holy Spirit, and I welcome You Holy Spirit in my life. But Father I know that there is more, so as You said in Luke 11:13 (KJV), "If ye then, being evil, know how to give good gifts unto your children: how much more shall your Heavenly Father give the Holy Spirit to them that ask Him?" I am asking You to fill me with the Holy Spirit. Holy Spirit rises up inside me as I praise God. I expect Father, as I praise Your name verbally, that I will begin to speak with other tongues as You give me the utterance, in Jesus's name.

I pray that the Lord will bless you and keep you, and that you will be forever changed.